Can Ethics Be Christian?

James M. Gustafson

CAN ETHICS BE CHRISTIAN?

WITHDRAWN

The University of
Chicago Press

Chicago and London

The University of Chicago Press, Chicago 60637
The University of Chicago Press, Ltd., London

Library of Congress Cataloging in Publication Data

Gustafson, James M
  Can ethics be Christian?

  Includes bibliographical references.
  1. Christian ethics. I. Title.
BJ1251.G86   241   74-11622
ISBN 0-226-31103-1

JAMES M. GUSTAFSON is University Professor
of Theological Ethics at the University of Chicago
Divinity School. He is the author of numerous
books, including *Theology and Christian Ethics*
and *Christ and the Moral Life.*

To   Karl Douglas and Katherine

             Greta Louise

             John Richard and

             Birgitta Maria

Contents

Preface

In 1967 I was invited by the Committee on the Shaffer Lectures of Northwestern University to address the question, "Is Christian Ethics Possible Today?" If I had focused on that, the lectures would have been sociologically oriented to a great extent. But a prior question had to be answered, a question I had pondered before the invitation and have since, namely, "In what sense can one speak at all of 'Christian' ethics?" That persons have spoken and written about Christian ethics is patently clear, but in the light of various philosophical positions and even some theological ones, another order of discourse seems in order. What is distinctive about Christian ethics?

The ramifications are many. For example, there are those who argue that ethics really does not permit "private" and "particular" historical or religious interests; ethics is ethics only when the basic criterion of judgment is whether all rational and disinterested persons could agree on the principles developed. Part of the problem is what can be legitimately included in ethical inquiry. In Christian ethics, particularly as that has been practiced by Protestants, one has a loose and extremely inclusive view of what is legitimate. When one is dealing with ethics in certain theological perspectives that inclusiveness is warranted; when Christian ethics (which has had in America a very practical purpose and history) is in the service of the churches it has involved empirical as well as theological and philosophical and biblical studies. I have not given an extensive theoretical justification for what I have done in this book; surely the assumption is that the realm of ethical inquiry is larger than many philosophers would permit. I have, however, sought to be self-critical in pressing the questions that I do.

The book begins with a brief narrative. The decision to do so was in part a practical one: the first audience included many undergraduates who were not particularly interested in my long-range purpose. The decision was based also upon a conviction that questions arise more provocatively when one starts with reflections on a particular human experience.

The text has been reworked many times, and has benefited from the critical reactions of readers and hearers at various stages. The first draft was written with the generous support of the Guggenheim Foundation during a leave from my duties at Yale University. Both stimulation and quiet were provided by Princeton University where I was a Post-Doctoral Fellow in the Department of Religion, and by the Reverend Rowland J. Cox and his family in whose home I resided. The most searching critical reading of the original lectures was done by Professor Donald Evans of Toronto. I have not met many of his trenchant philosophical criticisms; it would be a better book from some points of view if I had, but it would be a very different book, maybe not even my own. My former colleague William Christian responded in his generous and beautifully helpful way to the first draft of lectures. His spirit and method of inquiry I regard as a model worthy of emulation and as an inspiration for my work, though I never achieve his characteristic rigor; fortunately for me part of that spirit is to free one to work out his own approach. Professor Stanley Hauerwas, now of Notre Dame, also called me to account at many points in the first draft. At Northwestern, in April 1968, I received useful criticism from students whose names I never knew, and from Professors Manfred Vogel (who was my official host, and has become a friend), Henry Veatch, and Lawrence G. Lavengood. In various stages of development I have aired some of this material at the Methodist Seminary of Ohio, LaSalle University, Southeastern Baptist Seminary, Bethany Theological Seminary, at meetings of the New Haven Theological Discussion Group, the Carnegie Institute of Philosophy at Notre Dame, the College Theological Society of New England, and the Summer Institute of Philosophy at the Catholic University of America.

Julian Hartt, my former colleague in New Haven, now of the University of Virginia, has been a source of profound encouragement to me when I have despaired of the value of what I have written. He believes that there is an implicit core in my occasional articles addressed to many different questions, and in my previous books, and that it is worthwhile to reflect on that core more directly. This book does not fulfill what he thinks is worth doing, but it comes closer to it than my previous publications.

I recognize that many passages here require both more refined and more extensive treatment. I have limited my citations of sources and have not carried out arguments in the text or in footnotes with other writers. I offer what I have written as a modest contribution to an ongoing discussion out of which, I hope, there will come greater clarity about what "Christian ethics" might be.

1 Moral Dimensions of Experience

One way to begin an analysis of the various dimensions of ethical inquiry is to describe an incident from personal experience. The incident I shall use is, in some respects, a trivial one. The issues involved are not momentous in terms of their consequences for large numbers of people; nor do they touch anything as serious as the right to life. They are not as challenging as the problems of peace or social justice, nor as complex as these. Pedagogical value, however, the incident has, for it is likely to be closer to the normal sorts of experiences in which individuals have to make decisions every day than are many more socially significant moral issues. The experience I shall describe has the merit of convenience in that it is manageable in its proportions but opens up aspects of human experience analogous to those involved in more complex circumstances.

In the mid-1950s on a hot summer night a colleague and I had worked past midnight on a report marking the termination of a brief but intensive interdisciplinary study. We left our workroom in a midtown Manhattan hotel to go to the bar for some refreshment. Near us was seated a rather drunken young soldier, who proceeded to order another drink. He paid for it with a twenty-dollar bill, but my observing colleague noticed that the bartender gave him change for a five. My colleague insisted that the soldier receive the rest of his change. The bartender protested that the soldier had given him a five, and not a twenty-dollar bill. An argument ensued, and finally the bartender gave the soldier fifteen dollars, asserting that he was doing it only to keep peace in the establishment.

1

The soldier's inebriation progressed to the point where it was clear that he would soon "pass out." Certainly he was rapidly losing control of his speech and his muscles. My colleague talked to him as best one could in these circumstances and finally took the soldier's wallet from his pocket. There was identification indicating that the young man lived at a Long Island address. We took ten dollars from the wallet, and my colleague wrote a note indicating that we had done so, that we were putting him in a cab and giving the cab driver the ten dollars to take him home. He also gave our names and professions, and the telephone number of the hotel in which we were quartered by the corporation for whom we were doing the study. Thus the soldier or his family could make contact with us if they desired any further explanation.

We more or less dragged the soldier onto Lexington Avenue, where we hailed a taxi. My colleague gave the driver the ten-dollar bill and the address. He also took the driver's name and license number and indicated that we had the young man's name and address. Thus the driver knew that it would be possible to check out whether the drunken soldier had been delivered home. My colleague also informed the driver that we knew how much money was left in the wallet.

When the taxi drove off, we returned to the bar. The bartender was exclaiming that he had checked his funds and realized that it was a twenty the soldier had given him, and not a five. My colleague informed the bartender that he would speak to the hotel management about the incident in the morning and request that the bartender receive proper punishment. We retired to our rooms in the hotel.

If, as Wallace Stevens so beautifully makes clear, there are thirteen ways of looking at a blackbird, so one might twist and turn to get at least as many perspectives on this experience. Without seeking *a priori* certitude about whether this whole event was a "moral experience" or some other sort of experience, or even seeking to define the "moral dimensions" of this experience, it is possible to lift out of the account some of the characteristics of events and occasions in which persons make what they judge to be moral decisions, or engage in moral actions. One need not claim that this incident provides the occasion and sufficient data to give an account of the fundamental structure of human experience, or of the structure of persons; we need not leap to ontology to make some hopefully persuasive generalizations. At least to place the incident on another level, an abstract one, might indicate the ways in which it helps us to see some things that are characteristic of many incidents in our experience.

First, there is a describable network of relationships in this incident. The most significant relationships are between the soldier and the bartender, the bartender and my colleague, and my colleague and the soldier. These relationships might have existed without becoming the occasion for the series of actions and responses that occurred. If my colleague had not noticed that the soldier was given incorrect change, or if he had noticed it but passively concluded that the matter was none of his business, those relationships would not have developed in the way they did. Our intention was to refresh ourselves after an exhausting evening of composing a report; we did not go down to the street to seek out someone in need for whom we might do a service. We had not decided that we would engage in some moral action, or anything serious at all, before we retired. Rather, quite without our purposes we happened accidentally to be in a place during a brief time span in which a relationship between a drunken soldier and a bartender provided the setting for an act that could be described either as cheating or as a mistake. There followed the relationship of each man with my colleague.

What was it that made these relationships an occasion for the sorts of actions I have described? First, my colleague, an observant person, saw a transaction which was either a mistake or deliberate cheating. He surmised, on the basis of previous experience and knowledge, that the transaction was not a mistake (and therefore not accidental), but was cheating (and therefore intentional). He interpreted what he observed, though not self-consciously, and thus accounted for the significance of what he saw: that account involved a sort of moral judgment. His reaction was one of indignation; he had strong feelings about what he observed and understood to be going on. Something he judged to be morally wrong had occurred: a commonly accepted rule of moral behavior had been broken, namely, "Thou shalt not cheat." Or the rights of a person were being violated: the soldier had a right to his full change. Or a relationship of trust between persons was violated: the soldier had the confidence in the bartender one should normally expect, but the bartender was not trustworthy. Or a person who was not fully accountable for his behavior, here owing to his advanced drunkenness, was being taken advantage of: others have an obligation particularly to those who cannot fend for themselves.

The interpretation of what was going on in the circumstances was at once both descriptive and evaluative. Indeed, even the use of the word interpretation suggests more self-consciousness than was present in my colleague. Perhaps observation and interpretation were compacted into a perception that something morally wrong was occurring. It might be that only after certain events can one give a rational account of them. Of the act in question one might say, "When bartenders are dealing with people who are very drunk they are likely to cheat them. Thus be alert to this possibility when you are in bars." Or, it could be said that my colleague quickly saw that certain potential future consequences of a nonbeneficial sort were predictable unless they could be avoided by an intervention which directed the course of events in a different way. But surely in the moment there had been no such conscious and deliberate analysis. The moral issue he perceived took place within a set of relationships that were there. The relationships were not brought into being for the sake of the fulfillment of some moral purpose. But a descriptive evaluation of them or, if you prefer, an evaluative description of them, raised what my colleague perceived to be an occasion for intervention of a sort that was morally justified and, in his experience, mandatory.

Second, the relationships were of mutual reliance of persons upon each other. They were a web of interdependence in which individuals relied upon each other to be dependable, to fulfill their roles. When the soldier ordered his drink the bartender assumed that as a customer he had the money to pay for it and would not renege his obligation. In turn, the soldier assumed that the bartender would not violate his obligation as the seller and would give him correct change. Their obligations to each other were the obverse of their relationships of dependence upon each other in which each assumed the other to be dependable, reliable, trustworthy.

As the course of events unfolded, there was no such socially structured network of roles and mutual dependence and obligation. It is clear that the soldier was not in a condition to be self-reliant, and thus if his interests were to be protected he would have to rely upon others to assume certain roles. Indeed, one might say that his dependence upon others increased, but there were no specific persons with socially defined roles to assume obligations to him. Thus, in a sense, my colleague volunteered to assume the role of a person on whom the soldier could rely in order to protect him from further harm. Perhaps my companion thought, "The poor fellow really needs someone to help him, since he is in no position to help himself." He really was in a vague and general way dependent upon others, because he was losing his capacities for self-determination and self-reliance. Recognizing this, my colleague assumed the role of a person upon whom the soldier could rely because he felt an obligation to do so. He acted in such a way as to bring into being a new pattern of dependence and reliability, and by assuming a role in this pattern he accepted a set of obligations.

In the initial stages of the events the soldier and the bartender had the right to make explicit and defined claims upon each other. The claims were "built into" their respective roles in a relationship between seller and buyer. Claims arise out of relationships of mutual dependence; relations of mutual dependence are occasions for relations of mutual obligations. In the subsequent stages of events the dependence continued but was not specified in terms of conventional roles and therefore explicit claims. In a sense the soldier's need for help was responded to by my colleague in his assumption of the role of the reliable person. While the soldier did not have a claim upon him, as he had on the bartender, my companion felt the soldier's needs to be a claim upon him.

Third, the relations, obviously, were neither static nor passive. Interaction between persons was occurring. The issues perceived to be moral occur in interaction, in this case, between individuals.

The exchange of money for a drink provided the occasion for an action by the bartender which my colleague judged to be morally wrong. If the soldier had received correct change, which is to say that if the action of the bartender had been in accord with the moral obligations between a customer and a seller that are accepted as right, there would have been no occasion for my colleague's intervention at that time and place. If the bartender had been a trustworthy person, had obeyed the moral rules, had not violated the rights of the soldier, or had not sought to take advantage of him in his condition of drunkenness, we would have shortly left the bar as unobtrusively as we entered it. The interaction between the bartender and the soldier was alterable; either a mistake had been made that could be corrected, or deception had occurred that could be rectified. The sequence of interactions was not inexorable; it was not fated. Rather, at various points in the sequence human agency could be exercised in accordance with moral purposes to alter the course. Various persons could exercise capacities and powers available to them as means of intervention, and the media of such powers were several.

Speech was involved: the bartender was verbally accused of giving incorrect change, and he defended himself verbally. Money was used to attempt to insure the safety of the soldier by paying the driver to take him home. Muscular power was used to drag him from the bar to the street and into the taxi. These capacities, or forms of power, were used as means of intervention in a process of interaction. They were used in accordance with certain intentions and purposes, which were moral in the sense that judgments about what was right and wrong were brought to bear through their usage, and in the sense that the welfare of the soldier was the principal end to be achieved through other purposes and through various means. Choices were made about which capacities were the appropriate media for action and interaction in the particular circumstances in which we found ourselves. My colleague, for example, might have judged that there had been a violation of the law in the cheating, and thus he could have sought the police and filed a complaint or sought an arrest of the bartender.

The general point is this: the occasions for moral actions come into being in the processes of human interaction. Since these processes are not predetermined by some inexorable force of fate, it is possible to use available and appropriate capacities and powers in accordance with moral intentions or purposes to alter and even direct the course of subsequent interactions. The course of interaction on Lexington Avenue was altered by the capacities that my colleague exercised.

Fourth, it is obvious that what did occur in the interactions was in part dependent upon a past sequence of events, and upon the sorts of persons who participated in this occasion. There was a significant degree of determinacy present both in the circumstances and in the persons who participated. Certain limits were present, and certain potentialities were present, not because anyone chose them to be there, but because of the past. The bartender, for example, was the sort of person who would cheat a customer if he thought he could get away with it. We do not know enough about him to say that it was absolutely in character for him to cheat every chance he got; this might well have been the first time he engaged in such an act. His cheating of the soldier was an act to be sure: he exercised his role and capacities with the apparent intention to cheat. But he was also the sort of person whose moral beliefs, or whose absence of a sense of obligation to be honest, seemed to permit him to do what he did.

Not everyone sitting at the bar responded as my friend responded; the cheating probably was observed by others but did not lead to any intervention on their parts. Certain aspects of my colleague's experience and character were crucial in enabling him to initiate the sequence of events that he did. What he was as a person, the sorts of experiences he had had, what he knew about some bartenders, the "courage of his convictions," his indignation which was consistently evoked by all sorts of injustices—in short, his character was a necessary condition for the actions he undertook and for the course of events that followed. If he had not been the "sort of person" he was, the course of events would have been different. The admirable practical skill with which he acted suggests that he was not a novice to such experiences; he had probably helped other persons in similar circumstances. My own basic intention was probably the same as his, that is, to protect the interests and the welfare of the drunken soldier, but I was not the "sort of person" he was; I lacked the experience and the practical wisdom to act in such fitting ways as he did. If I had been there alone the sequence of events would have been different, and probably less commendable.

The circumstances of the soldier were also a necessary condition for the course of events as they occurred, though they were not in a strong sense determinative of it. If he had not been in such an advanced state of inebriation at the time we arrived, he could have protected his own interests. Indeed, the bartender might not have been tempted to deceive him but probably would have honored his rights without a warning or a threat. We do not know why the soldier was getting drunk on that summer night; there might have been some deeply unconscious motives stemming from parental or sibling relationships, or he might have been jilted by his date, or perhaps he was lonely, or maybe he believed that when soldiers get to Manhattan for an evening they have fun by getting drunk. All that lay behind the soldier's condition and circumstances, all the motives for it, do not matter in a significant way for the moral judgment that it was wrong for him to be cheated, or for the need to protect his welfare. But apart from them the occasion for moral decisions and actions would not have occurred. To be sure, a more intensive and extensive relationship with him might have been possible. We could have telephoned him the next day to see if we could be of assistance in counseling him so that he might avoid such occasions in the future. But the post-midnight hour on Lexington Avenue was not the time and place for that sort of relationship. What was required then and there was determined in part by a state of affairs and a prior sequence of events which no one of us, including the bartender, was fully accountable for creating. There were determinate circumstances and conditions which were necessary for the course of action to develop which did.

If my colleague had had different moral beliefs from those he did have, the sequence would have been different. What he did was in part an expression of certain moral convictions. If he had believed that drunks deserve what comes to them as a result of their drunkenness, he would have thought that the soldier was simply getting what was due him. If he had believed that bartenders were poorly paid and had a right to augment their income by cheating customers, he would have remained passive. Or more plausibly, if he had believed that he had no obligation to object to a moral wrong that he observed, even though he judged it to be wrong, he would not have intervened. The course of events would probably have been other than it was if he had not had certain moral beliefs.

A generalization seems to be warranted from this. What happens in the course of events in which moral interventions take place is dependent upon certain necessary conditions. These conditions set the limitations and create the possibilities of action. The conditions include the "sorts of persons" who are related to and interacting with each other; they include the specific circumstances of time and place, of affairs in which the interactions are occurring. Generally the agents do not "create" the circumstances out of which the occasions for action arise, nor do they have the capacities radically to "re-create" them. What the agents can actually do is conditioned by their own particular capacities; they cannot "re-create" themselves in the moment that action is possible. There are some things to which persons can only "consent," to use a term of Paul Ricoeur's. Such freedom as they have is "situated freedom," to use a term of Merleau-Ponty's. One further refinement is needed. It might, indeed, be more accurate to say that what a person intentionally does is determined in part by his *perception* and *understanding* of what the other person is, what the circumstances are, and what he and others can do. We *judge* what the state of affairs is, what others are intending, what the consequences are likely to be if we do not intervene, and if we do. But our perceptions, under-standings, and judgments are of and about determinate condi-tions which we are experiencing.

Fifth, the interaction and relationships were not absolutely determined; the state of affairs and the course of events were subject to alteration and redirection through the intervention of persons as they exercised their capacities in accordance with their purposes or intentions. It is true that the possibilities for action were limited by virtue of the relationships existing in that bar on that evening, and by the sorts of persons who were interacting with each other then and there. Nonetheless, there were also indeterminacies; there was openness which made intervention possible. The soldier was not "destined" to be cheated, to get so drunk that he passed out, to be "rolled" for his remaining money on the streets of New York. My colleague could speak on his behalf to the bartender; we could exercise our physical strength to get him safely into a cab. The course of events was not inexorable. My colleague was not fated to sit by in silence while observing an injustice any more than he was fated to intervene when an injustice was observed. The bartender decided to exercise his capacities in the transaction of money in accord with the intention to cheat; when it became clear to him that my colleague "meant business" in pursuing our efforts to rectify injustice and to protect the soldier from further harm, he exercised his capacities again to acknowledge that the bill he received was a twenty.

I could have done otherwise than I did in those circumstances, and if I had I would be in some degree a different person than I am now. I might have excused myself by saying that the whole thing was none of my business. Or I might have said that it is embarrassing for a person of clerical status to be involved in a dispute in a bar in Manhattan in the early morning hours, and hastened to my room. Or I could have observed the practical finesse of my colleague without assisting him. I chose, however, not to follow these possible courses of action. By participating with my colleague, I altered my own person in some ways. I have the memory of a sequence of events indelibly imprinted in my mind. My capacities for practical moral action were enlarged by sharing with an experienced artist of moral action; I know better now how to go about doing certain things in similar circumstances. By becoming a participant in this relatively insignificant affair I learned something about the importance of being active and participating in order to understand the complexities of experience and of its moral dimensions.

Thus, while there were features of the circumstances and the course of events that were unalterable (the soldier's drunkenness could not be quickly reversed to sobriety, for example), the course of events was alterable. There were points of openness, of indeterminacy in which capacities could be exerted to direct events in a limitedly different way. There was no "natural course" that was destined to be followed; the course was directed by the actions of the participants. As a result of actions, the circumstances and the persons involved became different from what they would have been had there been no intentional interventions. There was at least a modest "increment" of experience for each of us, more for some than for others. Even my skilled and wise colleague was able in a conversation some years later to recall, analyze, and reinterpret the significance of that time and place.

A sixth characteristic of this experience can be highlighted. The interactions occurred between one person and another; this can be stated in terms of self-other. There was also development of a sequence of events through a brief time span; this can be stated in terms of past-present-future. If one imagines these two dimensions superimposed upon each other, one can visualize the hyphens crossing each other:

	self			self	
past	+	present		+	future
	other			other	

The hyphens as they cross each other represent the openings, the occasions, and the interstices in which purposive action is possible. They represent the occasions in which the exercise of some capacity or form of power can make a difference to the sequence of events and to the circumstances of the persons involved. The monetary transaction between the soldier and the bartender was one such; it was an occasion in which the bartender could cheat or be honest. Because he cheated, the course of events took a different direction from what it would have taken if he had been honest. The observation of that act (of a particular way of crossing the interstice between self and other, and between past and present) led to my colleague's exercise of his capacities of speech to insist that correct change be given; this also made a difference in the course of events. Subsequently, as the soldier was passing out, a variety of possible interactions between himself and several others could have occurred. He might have been "thrown out" onto the street, where he might have been "mugged" for the rest of his money. But something else happened because in that moment we decided to use a variety of capacities in accordance with a general purpose to protect his welfare. We used our bodily strength to drag him to the street and to call a taxi; we used his monetary power to provide him transportation to his home address, where presumably he would be taken care of; my colleague used his capacities for speech to indicate to the driver that certain possible contingencies in the future course of events were, in a sense, averted by the sorts of information we had about the soldier (how much money he had left, for example) and about the driver.

In these interstices between self and other, and between past and present, and present and future, various capacities were exercised in order to give some determination to the subsequent course of events, and to the subsequent state of affairs. My colleague, with some assistance from me, used these occasions to protect the rights of the soldier and to seek what we judged to be most beneficial to him in the circumstances. We were able to meet obligations we felt we had to the soldier, and even to society; or, if you prefer, we were given certain opportunities to act in such a way as to avoid certain forms of evil that might have come into being had we not acted. The interstices, represented by hyphens, are the occasions for action.

Seventh, from this narrative a certain view of persons can be developed. Persons are not merely passive chips floating on rivers of events and circumstances and carried by whatever currents flow. Rather they are agents, or actors. They have capacities that can be exercised in accordance with moral purposes, moral rules, moral values, moral ends; they have access to forms of power, such as money, which can be used to alter or direct a course of events. As agents, they have capacities to determine themselves to some extent; they can intend to exercise their capacities in certain ways and can follow through on such intentions. They can reflect on what moral principles or rules apply ("Thou shalt not cheat"; "The rights of individuals ought to be protected"), on what ends ought to be achieved ("One ought to act in such a way that a minimum of harm or evil occurs"), on what values are at stake ("honesty"), and so forth. This reflection may take place in "the twinkling of an eye" (to translate literally the word for "moment" in Germanic languages), or it may be slower and more deliberative. In either case it enters into the determination of the agents' capacities and has consequences for the future course of events.

Perhaps a restatement of the points drawn from this experience will help to indicate those dimensions or aspects out of which developed distinctively moral activity.

1. Moral activity comes into being within relationships between persons and others. The other is usually another person. It might, however, in some circumstances be either directly or indirectly an institution like the state or a law or a course of events that is delineated as some kind of entity (the war in Vietnam), though persons are always involved in these as well.

2. The relationships are of mutual dependence, mutual reliability, and it is out of this mutuality that moral obligations and claims emerge. Sometimes the obligations are explicit in the roles that persons have in social structures, such as seller and buyer. At other times persons voluntarily assume the role of the person who is to be relied upon, and obligations are thus assumed.

3. The relationships are not static; interaction is occurring in them. The interaction provides the occasion for responses and initiations, for change, process, reform, revolution, or other exercises of influences and power. Interaction is the necessary condition for intentional alteration of states of affairs or courses of events.

4. The interaction is between "terms" which represent states of some determinacy: between persons or institutions that are actual, designatable, and limited. The actuality represents both limitations and possibilities of action. Persons have both limitations and capacities that are the consequence of "who they are," or their past experiences, their physical powers, learning, and courage. The "other" similarly presents both limits and possibilities of a relatively fixed sort.

5. There is, however, also a measure of indeterminacy in the "terms" that interact. The relationship between self and other can be altered through their actions on each other, and both the

self and the other are to some degree alterable as a result of such action. What "I am" is to some extent designatable, but as a result of action and interaction, I shall not be precisely what I am now. The other also has a malleability which makes it possible for him or her, or it, to become other than what it now is.

6. There are interstices between one person and another, and between the past, the present, and the future, in which capacities and powers can be exercised. They are the occasions in which intentional use of speech, physical power, money, votes, and so on can make a difference to persons, states of affairs, and courses of events.

7. Persons are agents; they exercise capacities and powers in accordance with purposes, for our concerns moral purposes. They can reflect upon these purposes and govern their exercise of capacities (which is to say they can act) in accordance with them.

These are generalizations about the fundamental conditions necessary for moral judgments, moral decisions, and moral actions to occur. As stated here they are cryptic. For those interested in ontology, they do not respond to the claim that something of the fundamental structure of reality, or even of human reality is here disclosed. For those interested in further specification of the relation of freedom and determinism, they are relatively imprecise and undeveloped at crucial points. I do not deny that a more probing and technical exploration and elucidation of them is required. Their introduction here has modest aim, namely, to render the experiences of persons in particular circumstances more intelligible by providing a framework for understanding them, and to suggest that this framework is likely to be meaningful and intelligible to other persons because it enables them to understand their own experiences in other circumstances.

They are not generalizations about *the* pattern, or *the* structure of moral experience. Indeed, it is possible to formulate, based on observations of the moral actions of persons, various descriptive generalizations, or various ideal-types of ways in which men live morally under these conditions. Different persons act character-istically as moral agents in different ways. This can be illustrated by suggesting some different answers that might be given to the question that pertains to the beginning of the events narrated, namely, why did a moral question come up at all in that bar? There are different sorts of answers that different persons would give to that question. These sorts of answers might suggest various patterns of "moral life."

A business transaction occurred, and the customer received the wrong change. On what grounds might different persons judge that to be morally wrong? What might some characteristic answers be?

One might be that the action was not in accord with a moral rule. Moral rules can be stated in such a way that they cover a large range of cases, or they can be stated more specifically. There might be an inclusive rule about obligations to be honest, which could be specified with reference to business transactions in terms of "Thou shalt not cheat." Perhaps something like this goes on quickly in the mind of the person who judges the act to be wrong: giving incorrect change can fit either one of two classes of actions; it is either a mistake, or it is cheating. In the circumstances in which it took place—a drunken customer and a midtown bartender interacting—one presumes that the bartender intended to give the wrong change; thus it is cheating. But it is defined as cheating because the bartender's intention and action were not in accord with the moral rule as they ought to be. Therefore the act was morally wrong.

Another sort of answer might be that the action violated a human relationship of trust. In the observer's mind something like this might occur. Human beings exist "in each other's hands," to make the point somewhat poetically, as Knud Løgstrup does. They are mutually interdependent, and in order to survive and be fulfilled in the relationship, they rely upon each other, they have confidence in each other, they trust each other. This trust is a necessary condition for their human existence. For this trust to be sustained there are other conditions; namely, those on whom they rely must be reliable and those in whom they trust must be trustworthy. If one presumes that the giving of incorrect change was intentional, it was a violation of trust, or of the conditions in which trust can be sustained. Thus it disrupted the relationships necessary for authentic human life to exist and is therefore morally wrong.

A third answer might not use the motif of trust so much as the motif of rights. What was violated was the soldier's right; he had a clear and unambiguous, indeed an unconditioned, right to his correct change. His right to justice was violated by the cheating. If justice means "to each his due," there is no question about what was due the soldier in this case, what he had a right to. If justice refers to "fairness," there is no question that the giving of incorrect change was unfair to the soldier, for the bartender appeared to assume that because of the soldier's particular drunken condition he did not have to treat him with the same respect, with the same sort of action, as he would treat other customers. Indeed, it was a violation not merely of the soldier's moral rights but also of his legal rights. And thus it was wrong.

A fourth sort of answer might have considered it wrong primarily with reference to its consequences, or its potential consequences, not only for the individual persons immediately involved, but for "society." The adverse consequences for the soldier were that he would not have the money he thought he had to spend on the next occasion when he needed it. For the bartender, his immediate interests were served by the cheating, but his long-range interests might not be, for if he was caught cheating customers, as he was, it might cost him his job, and perhaps also bring him under arrest. In his case, "honesty is the best policy" because it leads to the best consequences in the long run. For society, there is the prospect of increasing amounts of this sort of cheating so that the social fabric of the assumption of honesty in business transactions would be weakened. This could lead to increasing anxiety among persons, to the necessity for increasing vigilance in all relationships, and to the necessity for forms of enforcement which would be economically costly. Cheating is wrong because of the adverse consequences which it leads to.

A fifth answer might have judged it to be morally deficient rather than morally wrong if moral life was viewed as the highest possible approximation of certain moral ideals. Among the moral ideals would be that of a society in which all persons could be relied upon to be honest, for if such were achieved persons could live with greater equanimity, with a sense of confidence that others were reliable, and thus with greater freedom from anxiety. Such an ideal, it might be said, ought to be held by all persons, and all actions ought to approximate that ideal under all normal circumstances, or indeed under all circumstances. To cheat the soldier was far from the sort of approximation or fulfillment of the moral ideal, and thus was morally deficient.

Still another might say that the bartender's action was not a morally fitting one in those circumstances. A person might be willing to argue that in certain circumstances such cheating might be morally fitting, for example, if running out of money was the only way in which the soldier could be kept from harming himself by further drinking and other possible adverse consequences of drunkenness. Or he might argue that if the bartender's family were being deprived of the means of livelihood because of his low wages, there might be some justification for him to cheat customers who were foolish enough to get drunk so that he could better support his family. But in assessing the circumstances present that early mid-summer morning in that hotel bar in midtown Manhattan, the fitting response for the bartender would have been to give the soldier his correct change. Such an act would fit the "Gestalt" better than the cheating would.

Persons who make the judgment that the bartender's action was morally wrong in any one or any combination of the patterns I have suggested need not follow the same pattern or combination of patterns in deciding what they ought to do, or in acting on the basis of the decision. There might well be adherence to a rule that leads to the judgment that the cheating is wrong, and there might be action-guiding rules which determine that something ought to be done, and even to some extent what ought to be done. For example, if one observes a moral wrong, one ought to do whatever is necessary to rectify the misdeed. But there may be no clear rules governing the means of action which are morally appropriate to achieve that end, at least none that one could readily state prior to acting. To be sure, one ought not to do anything unjust to the bartender, but what sorts of action would be just to him are not easily covered by rules that can be generalized to cover many instances. One could say that whatever one decides to do here, one ought also to be ready to do in the same or similar circumstances, but it is not very often that one person would find himself in a position where the same circumstances occurred, unless, of course, he were a steady patron of bars. Thus, as one can interpret my colleague's action, there can be a shift to a pattern of "fitting" actions relative to rectifying the earlier injustice first and to insuring the fewest possible consequences adverse to the interests of the soldier subsequently. What my colleague immediately or intuitively perceived to be fitting courses of action might be justified by moral principles or rules on another level of discourse in a later moment of reflection, but what he did appears to reflect the moral virtuoso acting in accordance with a character formed through previous experiences and through the internalization of certain moral beliefs, values, or principles. The sort of person, or agent, he was, seems to have been more important in this instance than any processes of practical moral reasoning he had been trained to use, or, as a matter of fact, any processes of justification he could give for what he did after the sequence of incidents was over.

From this one might indicate certain "styles" of moral decision making or moral activity in an oversimplified way. One style might find its closest analogy in the model of law, either in the natural law or the common law tradition. In the natural law tradition, one would seek to determine what universally applicable principles and what second order principles fit the circumstances in hand. Then one would proceed to reason practically from these principles to determine in what way one ought to decide and to act in the present conditions. In the common law tradition, one would seek for precedents in previous experience of one's community which were set in the process of making judgments, deciding, and acting in cases similar to the one in hand. From these precedents one would find guidance in determining what ought to be done in the present time and place. This style would be what H. Richard Niebuhr called "man-the-citizen," who comes to "self-awareness if not to self-existence in the midst of *mores*, of commandments and rules, *Thou shalts* and *Thou shalt nots*, of directions and permissions."[1]

Another style might find its closest analogy in the model of engineering or building. One has a model or design in mind for the sort of society one wishes to build, or for the sort of person one wishes to become; one has an end in view. Then one proceeds to act in such a way that the design or model is fulfilled through a process of means-end thinking and acting. In order to actualize the design of justice in these circumstances the agent determines to take a series of steps, engage in a series of actions. This would be Niebuhr's image of an artificer "who constructs things according to an ideal and for the sake of an end."[2] It is the image of *homo faber* delineated by Hannah Arendt in *The Human Condition.*[3]

Niebuhr and Arendt each have another model. Both appear to believe that the other model is, in a sense, more distinctively human. Niebuhr calls his "man-the-answerer," or the "responder." In this "we think of all our actions as having the pattern of what we do when we answer another who addresses us."[4] The focus of self-understanding is that of "responsive beings," who act in accordance with their interpretations of what is happening to them, and who respond in a way that is "fitting." Persons here are understood to be those who in the first moment are "acted upon" and then respond to what they have seen or what has been done to them. They interpret the meaning or significance of what has been done, and then act upon others in a way that is fitting, that fits what is going on.

This model I would judge to be in important respects analogous to aesthetic experience. Deciding what one ought to do is a matter of acting in such a way that one's action is properly harmonious with the circumstances, or properly dissonant with the circumstances, depending upon what effect one is seeking to create. In some circumstances one might be called upon to create an accent point relative to the whole picture in which one is working; in others only a slight inobtrusive stroke of a brush is appropriate. But one decides what to do by perceiving a whole and then determining what one ought to do that is fitting or appropriate to that whole. Historical roots for such an aesthetic analogy can be found in the Platonist and Stoic traditions, and within Christianity in the ethics of St. Ambrose and St. Augustine.

To some critics, the model of responsive beings appears to give warrant for excessive passivity; it appears to license a view of moral decisions and actions that is pragmatic in the worst sense and that leads to a high level of "muddling through" at best. Hannah Arendt's model of man-the-actor emphasizes initiation more than response, though one ought to note that more positive forms of action are accounted for in Niebuhr's model as well. One of the key aspects of action which Professor Arendt stresses is its unpredictability; "processes are started whose outcome is unpredictable, so that uncertainty rather than frailty becomes the decisive character of human affairs."[5] Important in this is the concept of "process," which Arendt indicates did not come to full recognition in the ancient world. To be sure, process is involved in fulfilling a goal in the *homo faber* model, but when process is coupled with *action,* one sees how the consequences of initiation multiply beyond the immediate intention of the actor and beyond his capacities to control them. To modern ears, this view has an even more existentialist ring than Niebuhr's view of man as responsive being. The style is recognizable at present in many personal decisions that people make: they act in recognition that the consequences of their initiations are beyond their control but find justification in the "authenticity" of the act itself. It is also recognizable in many of the activities of radicals in the social sphere: they have no clear picture of the order they are seeking to achieve, nor do they feel bound to follow accepted laws and customs; rather, they exercise their powers in the recognition that a process might be begun which will multiply its effects through a course of future events.

A model which in some respects might be distinguished from the previous ones is analogous to human experience in the sphere of economic productivity. Like some of the others, it is concerned for the consequences of actions, but it does not have such a clear design as does the teleological, nor is it focused on the fitting as is the aesthetic. It views moral action as the generation of consequences judged to be good, that is, to be of moral value, and the avoidance of consequences judged to be evil. Man is, in a sense, in the enterprise of producing effects, and he has to weigh the effects that he has produced, or those he ought to produce in terms of "cost-benefit" analysis. This is classically the utilitarian model. When the measurable harm that actions cause is greater than the measurable good, they are judged to be either morally wrong or morally deficient. In proposing certain actions, one is necessarily engaged in the hypothetical calculation of the values and the harms that might result. Consequences and potential consequences are converted into quantitative terms, and in the weighing of the quantities of "values" one is led to a judgment or a decision.

Perhaps there are other "styles" of moral decision making and action as well.[6] The condition of agency is necessary for any moral action, and thus it can be developed according to any of these patterns. If one attempted to fit the activity of my colleague in the bar into any of these styles, perhaps Niebuhr's man-the-responder comes closest. The fact that what my colleague did was commendable in my judgment does not make the style or pattern morally normative; we are here giving a descriptive typology without judging which one *ought* to be followed by all persons under most or all conditions. It might be the most normal, in the sense that its use is most common, though we have no statistical evidence that this is the case. There are those who would evaluate it as being the most "mature" way to act; and there was a virtuosity about his activity which evokes wide admiration. One could proceed to explore his actions and the general style that they fit. If one admires that sort of moral action and admires the sort of person who can engage in it, what would one have to do to become capable of comparable deeds? What sorts of moral education and formation, what sorts of experiences and beliefs, what sorts of sensibilities make that sort of person doing those sorts of things possible? To raise these questions opens the door not only to the practical issues but to philosophical issues as well. How is moral character to be understood? What is the relation between the sort of character one has and the sort of actions he engages in? How is the process of decision to be understood in such a case? Is it a "perceptual intuitionism"? And so on.

I will not completely disengage the subsequent discussions in this volume from the practical and philosophical questions, though it is not the purpose of this book to explore them technically and fully. Rather, the purpose is to explore certain religious dimensions in the moral dimensions of experience. This may seem to be an odd sort of move to make from the present discussion. My colleague was not a religious man in any traditional sense; he once stated that he had no use for ministers "unless they are socially useful" and could name some whom he admired on those grounds. He was not a reflective man; it was not part of his pattern of life to sort out the reasons which would justify his actions, or to reflect upon the patterns of them. His actions on that evening were not untypical of his life; he was engaged in many activities professionally, both as a lawyer and as a social worker, which were "in character," and his extraprofessional activities were almost totally of a morally "useful" sort. If he were a practicing, believing Christian one might ask what religious beliefs, training, loyalties, and disciplines seemed to be formative of his person and his actions. But he was not. Because he was not, he might be the occasion for a theological puzzle which could be resolved after many intricate theological moves by designating him an "anonymous Christian." He would not, however, have been honored or pleased with the appellation, nor would he have been impressed with the intellectual powers and the felt need that would lead to such a conclusion. His existence makes mockery of any pious attempts to show that in order to be morally commendable one has to be religious, and even tracing his history back to a Baptist Sunday school at the turn of the century looks like an apologetic trick, and an unpersuasive one at that. He would find nothing particularly "Christian" or even religious about what he did: its motives, its patterns of action, its consequences.

Why then use this narrative and this person as a starting point for exploring some of the religious dimensions in the experiences of men? One reason is that it affords the necessary conditions for moral action and for a discussion of the styles of decisions and actions which is not tinged with religious and theological overtones. The conditions and styles I have delineated are free from the overtones of religion and theology; the task of developing certain religious dimensions must be done in relation to patterns which are not confined to the lives of religious persons and communities. If the account thus far is free of religious overtones, it is pertinent to ask why such might be introduced for exploration. Why not proceed with a philosophical analysis devoid of theological language and claims? Such analysis would be appropriate, no doubt, and even in the development of a theological analysis, further reference will be made to philosophical issues. But the reason for turning to religious and theological dimensions which might be applicable is a professional one; I am a student of religious ethics, and particularly Christian ethics, and so certain questions pertinent to the narrative emerge with a Christian frame of reference. In taking an instance in which there are no overt religious and theological influences, one has to be somewhat harder headed about developing a discussion pointing to what influences religion and theology could have on moral agents, on the justifications for making decisions, and on the particular decisions themselves. In a sense, the subsequent chapters deal with the following question: If I had been the primary agent (or the hero of the story) in this sequence of events, what might have been the religious bases for what I was as a person, and for what I decided and did? Further, if my colleague and his actions were commendable (and I affirm that they were) without necessarily providing an authorative set of norms and patterns, what aspects of Christian life and thought might be important in enabling people to become something like my colleague, and to do something like what he did?

Thus the subsequent chapters have a double importance. One is to develop an intelligible interpretation of aspects of moral agency and action in the light of Christian life and beliefs. If a Christian had done what my colleague did, is there any basis in Christian life and thought which would make for a specially accented account of moral life? The other is to develop some positive moral claims on the basis of Christian life and thought: if one is conscientiously a Christian, why ought he to be or, less strongly, why might he be justified in becoming something like my colleague, doing something like the things he did?

In developing some answers to these questions, it will be necessary to move away from this narrative, for issues of a more general character require attention. But it will be possible to return occasionally to the narrative as a "reality check" on the more analytical and speculative accounts. Also it is hoped, as I indicated at the beginning of the chapter, that the reader will be able to identify sufficiently with the narrative and its actors to be stimulated to engage in his own reflections concurrently with reading mine.

2
The "Sort of Person" One Is

Ten years after the incident described in the first chapter, I met for the first time a distinguished woman who had been a professional colleague of my companion for a number of years and who was both his ardent admirer and close friend. We reminisced together about his life and career, for he was by then deceased. I told her about the experience at the bar. Her spontaneous response was, "That's just what you would have expected him to do." Her comment presents a puzzle to be solved, though all of its philosophical and psychological dimensions cannot be developed. Why is it that we can say of some persons after they have acted, "That's just what you would have expected him to do?" Or, perhaps on another occasion we might say, "I wouldn't have expected him to do that!" This merits some reflection.

One might say that the woman's comment was appropriate because my colleague was consistent in his responses and actions. This is an inference that can be drawn from observation of his words and deeds over an extended period of time. Consistency implies the expectation that in particular circumstances his responses and actions would be predictable, and those who knew him would be surprised if he said or did something different from what they expected. The term consistency, of course, is used most precisely in reference to statements and propositions. One can judge an argument, for example, in terms of its logical consistency. It is more difficult, and no doubt less precise, to speak of a consistency of responses. Perhaps all one can claim is that, in certain circumstances, a person usually gets indignant, or usually expresses moral approbation. Or when a certain person observes infractions of justice, he usually objects to them. When a person is judged to be consistent in his actions, what is meant is that there is a high degree of probability that he will act in predictable ways in certain situations. One might also be willing to deduce from this that there are certain identifiable characteristics of the person which predispose him to act in a highly predictable way. He might have certain "sensitivities," such as to injustice, which are, in a sense, "activated" when he observes cheating.

One might also develop the same point by saying that the person acts "in character." He does certain things so frequently that it is characteristic of him to do them; it would be "out of character" for him to do otherwise in similar circumstances. Observation of his activity over an extended period of time might lead to the assertion that "he is a man of character." More precise observations might lead to a specification of what "kind of character" a person has; my colleague was a man of compassionate character, or of courageous character. Here the reference would seem to be primarily to certain predispositions that he had, which would be evoked in certain relationships. But one also uses the notion of character to refer to predictable purposes or intentions that a person appears to have. To say that a person has character might refer to the observation that his actions appear to be governed by certain dominant purposes, or dominant intentions. For example, to say that a person is "loving" might suggest less that he has some predisposition toward emotions than that in action he generally tends to perform deeds that bring into being what might be characterized as relations of love.

Someone might say that my colleague was a man of great moral "integrity." The term, again, refers to consistency or predictability of response and action, for if in similar circumstances he always did different things, the word integrity would not come to mind as appropriate. Indeed, someone might say that he had no integrity at all. When the word "integrity" is qualified by the adjective "moral," something particular is pointed to. It might refer to an allegiance of the person to certain moral principles. For example, someone who is scrupulously honest even in circumstances in which his honesty is very costly to himself would be considered a person of high moral integrity; the moral principles or rules which prescribe honesty are consistently obeyed by that person. Moral integrity might refer to certain moral values that the person holds; if he highly values justice in the social order, and if his activities are generally in pursuit of justice wherever gross inequalities are visible in the society, one would not hesitate to call him a man of integrity. Or, the point that determines integrity might be an ideal vision a person has of himself; he would feel that he had compromised himself if he did not seek to live up to that ideal vision in all circumstances. In all these examples we see that integrity is, in a sense, a relational rather than substantive term; one's person and activities are integrated by or around some moral principles or values or ideals.

Perhaps what I have said suggests more self-consciousness than actually is the case in thoroughly "integrated" persons. Only through a process of drawing inferences from the actions of a person would one be able to determine what his principles, ideals, or values were. This might very well be a reflective procedure that the person had not gone through himself. Quite a different approach might be taken; one might find that a person's attitudes, habits, and even emotional responses seemed to be of a "whole piece," that is, they seemed to be integrated. The point of reference would appear to be not so much objective, such as principles which the person could articulate, but more subjective. There appears to be an "inner integrity," a wholeness which is commendable, not merely because it is integrated, but also because it is formed by some profound moral beliefs and commitments. These can, or course, refer to values and so forth that can be articulated, but on the face of it the beliefs and values which give the "color" to the integrity are so deeply "internalized" that the wholeness of a person's attitudes, emotional sensitivities, and habits is what strikes one first.

In the past decade another term came to be used to refer to predictability and consistency, namely, life-style. The notion of style can be used in a relatively morally neutral way; it is a generalization about patterns of behavior which one might or might not admire. But it does assume a wholeness; it is used, for example, to refer to persons whose speech, manner of dress, personal decorum, attitudes, and actions, all hold together in some way. In the 1950s, for example, one could meaningfully speak of a "Madison Avenue" style; this conjured up an image of gray flannel suits, white button-down-collar shirts, commuters, persons working hard to persuade others through manipulating their feelings, and so forth. In the sixties the notion of a "hippie" style had a similar communicability. The use of the term style to describe a person is roughly analogous to its use in histories of culture; there is a "baroque" style evoking elegance of dress, the dainty precision of the minuet, ornate patterns of decoration and art, the music of Vivaldi and Bach, and much more.

But the notion of "style" has also been loaded with evaluation. When President Kennedy was said to have had "style," the term referred not merely to a pattern of his life but to an evaluation of excellence. There was something, his admirers said, that lifted him above the ordinary politician: an elegance, a sharpness of wit, an appreciation for culture, an ability to have wide impact on the public.

The notion of style, when it refers to a moral manner of life, sometimes blends the descriptive and the evaluative references. Some Christians, for example, talk about a Christian "life-style." They mean, I believe, not only to refer to a wholeness that is visible through the manners and activities of Christians, but also to weigh this with a great deal of positive value. An element of exhortation is present in the use of the term; the lives of Christians ought to have certain characteristic attitudes, out-looks, dispositions, and actions; these are roughly describable, and are commendable.[1]

All these terms—consistency, character, integrity, style—suggest that it is appropriate to assume some degree of predictabil-ity of behavior in persons. There are persons whom we expect to do certain things in certain circumstances. If these persons act "out of character" we are provoked to try to explain why; indeed, we might even make excuses for such an action. We might use it as a basis for an inference about the person himself: he must have altered his beliefs or his moral commitments, or he must have access to information that we do not have which has led him to the unexpected behavior. Or there must be other reasons for his having done as he did which overrode the expected consistency of his actions. Or, by way of excuses, we might say that he must be tired or he had a hard day or lost a fight in a committee or has trouble in his family.

This possibility of predicting response and action is based on a common sense assumption that human actions are "caused," and that they are caused in part by the "sort of person" one is. Each of us makes this assumption about roommates, colleagues, friends, teachers, and students. It is assumed, for example, when professors are asked on recommendation forms for prospective graduate students to "characterize" the candidate's academic performance and sometimes even his personality. The warrant for the assumption is that the candidate's performance in graduate school is likely to be similar to his performance in college because the same "causes" of his actions will continue to be operative. Occasionally the only characterization one can give of a student is that he is predictably unpredictable!

Whether, in what sense, and precisely how actions are "caused," either by the sorts of persons we are or by other factors, is a matter of continuous debate. The door is opened to the historic free-will and determinism debate with its apparently endless restatements, and almost innumerable pages of argumentation.[2] The discussion persists as to whether human actions are satisfactorily explained on the basis of a "Hume-an" mechanistic view of causality, whether Kant's distinction between the phenomenal and noumenal aspects of the person is the basis for a better explanation, or whether new concepts are needed. A recent treatment of the issues, for example, distinguishes between "the continuous ingredience" of the self as agent and its "discontinuous ingression."[3] One finds general distinctions between "hard determinism," "libertarianism," and "soft determinism." One of the forms the debated question takes is whether human action is best explained by past-oriented causes or by future-oriented intentions and purposes. At stake is the degree of accountability that can be ascribed to persons for their own actions. At stake also is whether the spectator's or the agent's point of view is the proper one to take in explaining action, for often what looks caused from the external observer's point of view appears to be an act of self-determination from the agent's.

The issue was introduced in the discussion of the narrative in the previous chapter. There I raised the question of what might have "caused" the soldier to get drunk and what might have caused my companion to intervene actively. I indicated that the course of events was not inexorably fated, but that my colleague could intervene in accordance with purposes and intentions to alter it. Indeed, the concept of the person as agent implies that the capacity for self-determination in accordance with purposes is a necessary condition for moral activity. But at no point was a radical "libertarian" view of persons suggested as being plausible.

The issues are extraordinarily difficult to sort out with precision because of their complexity and interconnectedness, and because the terms used are subject to different definitions and usages. This can be illustrated briefly. Chaplain William Sloane Coffin of Yale is the "sort of person" who generally is engaged where there are significant issues of social justice and peace; his activities in the civil rights and peace movements are examples of this. One can say that Mr. Coffin is "motivated" to act whenever such social problems come to his attention. Indeed, one might say that he had "humanitarian" and "religious" motives. To what does the word "motive" refer when we use it this way? We can see how difficult it is to answer that question by referring to a standard dictionary definition of motive, as R. S. Peters does in his own study of the difficulties of *The Concept of Motivation.*[4] The Oxford English Dictionary defines motive as "that which 'moves' or induces a person to act in a certain way; a desire, fear, or other emotion, or a consideration of reason, which influences or tends to influence a person's volition; also often applied to a contemplated result or object the desire of which tends to influence volition." If we wish to explain Mr. Coffin's religious motives for his social actions, do we intend to refer to some religious *emotions* he has, or to religious *reasons* he might give for acting as he does, or to the *object* or goal of his action? The definition would permit attention to each of these, and it is possible that they are somehow related to each other.

In the tradition of Roman Catholic philosophy and theology, with its roots in Aristotle, the term "habit" has been used to account for persisting tendencies to act in characteristic ways. A distinction is made between what have been called motor habits, those which become automatic reflexes, and habits of the sort in which there remains some conscious determination of actions. For example, the University of St. Louis Thomist Klubertanz, in his extended discussion, offers the following summary definition of a habit of this second sort: it is "a quality which determines an operative power which is in some sense indeterminate, so that an ordered operation flows from that power with ease, consistency, and pleasure."[5] This is surely a different account of a habit from what a neurophysiologist would give, partially because he would be attending more to motor habits. Klubertanz's definition is morally neutral; it is presupposed in speaking about virtues, which are habits directed toward man's proper ends, and vices, which are habits directed toward improper ends. The problems are complex, and to get agreement on terminology is difficult. When we turn to the question of how religious life might affect motives or habits, we will complicate matters further. But if we are to make an intelligible account of that, it is necessary first to attempt to give an intelligible account of what underlies predictability of response and action.[6]

There are many factors for which we are not accountable that enter into becoming the "sort of person" each of us is: my colleague in the bar was, to use the dramatic language of some contemporary philosophers, "thrust into existence." More prosaically, this means at least that he did not choose to be, but came into being as a result of the biological processes of sexual intercourse; he could not choose his parents, but had to accept the genetic endowment that was his as a result of the genetic makeups that were theirs; he did not choose to live in the twentieth century with all of its technology, its wars in which he participated, its urbanization; he did not choose to be an American; he did not choose to be raised in a family of Christian Baptist religious persuasion; and so on. All these and many more factors were to him accidental in the sense that they did not occur as a result of any purposes or intentions of his own. These

accidents were in a sense to him matters of necessity or deter-
minateness, since there was nothing he could do to alter most of
them. To be sure, as he matured he could consent to and even
affirm some of them; to others he could dissent and could
minimize their significance in the process of his personal and
social development. He did not choose to emigrate from the
United States, and he did choose to disaffiliate himself from
religious institutions, but the processes of socialization and
formation in his earlier years took place in certain social contexts
without his consent or dissent.

From some points of view it is of no significance for understanding the moral dimensions of experience to take these factors
into account. In a special sense I would concur with the opinion
that it is meaningful to speak of morality only at those stages of
development and in those circumstances where a degree of
self-determination is possible, when a person can be held accountable for what he does. Yet, if the person's individual
capacities provide conditions in and from which his moral actions
occur, there is merit in at least briefly examining the bodily,
socio-cultural, and psychological "givens." If to some extent our
actions flow from the sort of persons we are, one needs to
recognize the significance of aspects of persons over which we
have limited or no control.[7] The fact that certain persons are
"excused" for certain infractions of law and morality recognizes this and provides an invitation for some exploration.

Those aspects of persons that most frequently excuse conditions for any moral wrong a person might have done are three.
One is the effects of a person's genetic endowment. While the
degree of precision in which relationships between genotype and
overt behavior can be drawn is at the present time minimal, there
can be no doubt that one's genotype in interaction with one's
environment (in the broadest sense) is one of the determinants of
one's phenotype. Capacities for physical and intellectual development are in part genetically dependent; susceptibilities to certain
physical and mental diseases are related to our genetic endowments. The lack of precision in understanding the relationship of
genetic endowment to behavior has made only the existence of the
XYY chromosome with its relation to aggressive behavior a

matter of public and legal discussion. Yet there are genetic conditions that are necessary, though not sufficient, for all sorts of morally approvable as well as condemnable action. One would not expect, for example, that a mongoloid person would have the same capacities as "normal" persons would to think through a complex ethical issue and come to a rational decision. Most persons would judge a mongoloid to be morally responsible only within vaguely defined limits of his capacities. Now it might well be that the capacities of "normal" persons to engage in practical moral reasoning, to be sensitive to issues of justice and injustice, to be concerned for the needs of others, and to act courageously are determined to some extent by their genotypes as well.

One can do nothing about one's genotype; it is the most "given" aspect of what a person is. But what one becomes with given genotype is a matter of the sorts of interactions one has with his physical, social, and cultural environments. His genotype, unless he is an identical twin, is unique; it fixes certain conditions both of limitations and of possibilities of development with which he lives. It is clear, however, that within those limitations both accidental and purposeful interactions make a difference to the sort of person he becomes. While at the present time it is not possible to say of a "normal" person that his concern for the well-being of others, or his lack of concern, is genetically determined, the possibility that his genetic endowment might be a factor of some significance remains open. Certainly insofar as the moral actions sometimes involve the maximal uses of one's bodily strengths, such as in restraining someone intent upon murder, and insofar as one's capacities for physical development are set by his genotype, the sorts of actions one has the capacity to do are dependent upon aspects of his life over which he has limited or no control. Whether a person's latent capacities are maximally or minimally developed is a matter only partially susceptible to his purposive actions. If, for example, he lives under conditions in which it is not possible to have the diet he needs, he cannot be held accountable for limitations in his physical capacity to act.

Does a person have a moral obligation to develop all his latent capacities to their fullest possible realization? It does not make sense to answer that in the affirmative, since various capacities are developed in relation to other persons, to particular circumstances in which one lives, and in response to the events and opportunities that one confronts. Capacities we have as a result of our genotypes are relatively undifferentiated, and to have a sense of obligation to develop all the possibilities of one's genotype would be impossible to fulfill even if it were a worthy feeling. But that the sort of person one is depends upon his genotype and that he cannot be held accountable for his genotype are both beyond doubt.

The second excusing condition for actions judged by others to be immoral is severe psychiatric illness. Just as a crude line is drawn between the normal and abnormal with regard to genetic endowments, so also is one drawn between the normal and the sick person in this regard. When one seeks to appeal to psychiatric illness as an excuse for legal or moral accountability, such a line must be drawn. To say the least, as the roots of human behavior have progressively come to be understood, both morally and legally some persons are no longer held responsible for what they do in various circumstances. Even the old and common assertion, "he is out of his mind," indicates that in folk wisdom a distinction has been drawn between the "mental" conditions under which a person can determine what he says and does and those under which he cannot. The controversy that ensues in almost every major trial in which psychiatric judgments are offered as excuses—for example, the trial of Sirhan Sirhan for the murder of Senator Robert Kennedy—points to the difficulties of precise determination of the degree of accountability for intentions and acts. If controversy exists in the courts, it exists also in the realm of moral judgments.[8]

In reflecting upon the person as a moral agent, there is a strong temptation, and there are good reasons for it, to sweep under a rug the whole matter of "unconscious motives." It has been argued with some cogency that the terms used, the concepts employed, are vague and imprecise, and that in the end it is not clear to what they refer. It has been argued that whatever they do refer to is essentially "pre-moral," and thus reflection on morality begins only at the point where one can give reasons for his intentions. It has also been argued that appeals to unconscious motives might give a kind of explanation for one's actions, but it is never a justification for actions. The task of ethics, it is said, is to understand the justifications, the ethically defensible reasons, one would give for what he does. I would find it convenient if I could readily agree with such arguments, for it is clear that we do not know enough about the precise relationships between what has been called "the unconscious" and particular actions to give definitive answers to questions raised by critics.

It is difficult to ignore the sorts of evidences that Erik Erikson gives, for example, for a relationship between various childhood experiences and the capacities that persons have to be loving, to be trusting, and to be hopeful.[9] Certainly it is more difficult to ignore Erikson's insights than it is to ignore the theological claim put forward by the theologian of hope, Jürgen Moltmann, that belief in the resurrection of Jesus Christ is the ground of hope.[10] Such a learned theological argument can be trivially reduced to the exclamation, "If I can believe in that, then nothing is impossible!" As a theologian I do not wish to ignore theological grounds, but even a theological argument has to take account of those mysterious and only vaguely comprehended recesses of persons which determine to some extent the outlooks and attitudes they have. It could be said, of course, that whether one's attitudes of lovingness, trustfulness, and hopefulness are grounded in the "unconscious" or in belief in the resurrection of Jesus Christ makes no difference for ethical inquiry, since such attitudes and outlooks are, again, "pre-moral." But, as the reader by now sees, a sharp distinction between the pre-moral and the moral is in the end rejected.

My companion in the Lexington Avenue bar engaged in actions which, to use Klubertanz's descriptive language cited above, flowed with ease and consistency, and perhaps even with pleasure from his powers and capacities. The source from which those actions flowed escapes thorough and detailed knowledge; the degree to which he could not have done otherwise than he did, that is to say the degree to which his actions were predetermined, can never be precisely delineated. Yet a reasonable but vague hypothesis can be suggested, namely, that his "unconscious" was as much a source of his actions, which were laudable, as it is the source of illegal and immoral actions of other persons whom we readily excuse on such grounds. If that might be the case, then a reflective account of what goes into becoming the sorts of persons we are must acknowledge the import of the "unconscious."

The third excusing condition, even more controversial, in part because it is more complex, is that the social and cultural environment conditions persons in ways for which they are not accountable. The assertion that "each man is the author of his own acts," if it is made with a strong emphasis on "author" and without much refinement, no longer carries the same degree of persuasiveness as it did to some people in the past. But a counterassertion that "society" is the author of each man's acts is equally implausible. We do not expect all Americans to act in the same way in the same circumstances; we do not expect all Catholics or Jews to do so, or even all members of the same family. Yet in an unsophisticated way, for example, the actions of an American in a foreign culture are often excused because they are attributed to his national origins, or to introduce a notion that is the subject of much controversy, because he shares in the "American character."

The social psychological accounts of the relations of "mind" and "self" or of "character" to society are varied to some extent. But among social scientists there is at least a general agreement on the vague proposition that what individuals are is in part the result of their interactions in particular cultures, and that they have internalized the beliefs and values of those cultures through language, symbols, and other media of communication such as gestures. Whether there are universal values, values that are found in every human culture, is a matter under debate. The extent to which men share some values in common as a result of their "natures" as human beings is a philosophical issue that has thus far defied an answer acceptable to "all rational men."

The precise relationships between the socially held values, the value preferences, and the outlooks of individuals in the same society and the behavior of these individuals have not been mapped out in detail, and perhaps can never be because of the number of variables involved. But certainly there is no dispute that participation in a particular society and culture has many effects on moral actions. The many cross-cultural studies by ethnologists and others demonstrate that the moral rules of various societies differ both in their content and in their force of obligation, that the values of different cultures dispose persons to different moral outlooks and preferences of action. With the increasing degree of tolerance in American society, members of one "subculture" do not expect members of another to conform to the same moral rules, to act in accordance with the same moral values. The fact that others were "raised differently" becomes a condition which excuses them for conforming to the moral rules that we might hold for ourselves.

To seek to assess accurately how the social conditions of my colleague's childhood, and of his adult life, influenced his words and deeds near the end of his career is a task beyond human capacities to know. The relationship between the social structures in which he had participated and his character defy precise analysis. Whether religious and moral beliefs that were part of his family were more important in forming his compassion and courage than were certain significant experiences of personal interaction is impossible to judge. To engage in such a game of analysis is comparable to what a book reviewer sometimes does with his text. He knows that the author grew up in a certain region, or in a certain type of family, and it makes sense to him to attribute to what the author wrote some influence from this background, but just what it is beyond certain expressions of language is beyond analysis. Or, to cite the burnt over territory of the "Weber" thesis about the relationship between the "Protestant ethic" and the "spirit of capitalism," there seems to many persons to be an "affinity" between the two, but whether the ethos of Protestantism was historically more significant in its causality than the emergence of technology, the development of new banking systems, and the like is a matter that will continue to be subject to debate. Even to make a minimal claim that a certain sociocultural background was a condition for the emergence of my colleague's character and activity is difficult to "prove" in a strong sense. Yet, it remains plausible to assert that the sort of person he became was in part determined by the culture in which he lived, by the social structures in which he participated, through a process of "internalization" of the meanings and values in his society.

There is another range of terms much discussed in philosophy that focus upon why one might say after observing a person, "That's just what you would have expected him to do." These are the terms belief, disposition, and intention. Whether "affection" should be treated on the same plane of seriousness as these other terms or subordinated to them seems to be uncertain. Since it is as important to develop an intelligible account of the relations to each other of what these terms refer to as it is to render accounts of each independently, our task is complex.[11]

We might look for the "cause" of the predictability of a person's actions by examining his beliefs. We might say that a person acts with a great deal of consistency in certain sorts of circumstances because he believes in certain things, or believes that certain things are true or valuable. We expect physicians to seek to heal the sick, for example, not only because that is their role in society but also because they believe in the value of human physical life, or because they believe that physical life is of value. One sees immediately that it is necessary to move forward to indicate how some of the other terms listed apply. Because the physician believes in the value of physical life, he is *disposed* to seek to preserve it in most circumstances, and *intends* (both in his consciousness and in his will) to achieve those ends which will preserve it. We would be surprised to find a physician who acted frequently to destroy rather than to preserve human life. If he believes in the value of physical life, a certain general course of action is predictable because it is consonant with his belief.

A person's beliefs might be judged to be morally reprehensible because the actions that are informed and guided by them are consistently morally bad, indeed evil. For example, anti-Semitism was a belief of the Nazis, which led to a course of action with fervent consistency. There was a correlation between certain beliefs stated in documents and in propaganda with the dispositions of the believers to be hostile to Jews and with the declared intentions of many of them to eliminate as many Jews as possible. While the fervor with which the holocaust was pursued was also a function of authoritarian personality characteristics, so that an Eichmann could plead that he was only following the orders of his superiors, the same characteristics informed by different beliefs would have clearly led to other actions. The same passion, informed by a belief that all human beings are due a maximum of basic respect, would have led to a course of action that would not have been judged morally reprehensible. Indeed, such a belief would be held to be morally commendable because a course of action consistent with it would have led to consequences which most men would approve.

This illustration suggests that one must note not only differences in beliefs but also differences in "believing." A particular belief can be held with different degrees or sorts of conviction or commitment; all beliefs are not believed in with the same degree of intensity. Many Americans "believe" that all men are created equal, but not all find that belief to be significant enough to orient their actions toward others, to develop their stance toward social institutions, and to bother to bring it to bear on particular decisions. Their convictions about that belief are weak; there is no commitment on their part to it. Indeed there are some things we can be said to believe which (at least in our time) require no great emotional, passionate assent, such as "I believe the earth is round." In a sense we are saying, "I assent to the proposition 'the earth is round'; I assent to its truth." There are others which have different significance for dispositions and actions depending upon the extent to which they are passionately assented to, or depending upon the extent to which persons are "committed" to them. Belief in justice, for example (granting that the term means different things to different persons), will have one sort of impact on the attitudes and actions of persons if they give superficial verbal assent to the belief, and another if it is a belief which has convicted or convinced them, or one to which they have made a commitment.

It is also true that one gives tacit consent to many "beliefs" which might well inform one's moral action. The nineteenth-century theologian and preacher Horace Bushnell could write about the "unconscious influences of grace"; in a comparable way one might speak of the "unconscious influences" of certain beliefs, and of "tacit beliefs" from which certain directions for action come without either awareness of the "belief" or of the ways in which it influences us. One might infer from the consistency of actions of a person that he seems to believe, for example, in justice, though the person seems not to have articulated such a belief and is not conscious of its informing and directing significance for his actions.[12]

I have noted that my companion at the Lexington Avenue bar was not a particularly reflective person. I doubt if he could have given a ready answer if one had asked him, "What do you believe in?" Perhaps his beliefs were tacit; perhaps he never articulated them and had never expressed a commitment to them. Nonetheless, the inference might be warranted that there were certain moral beliefs or convictions that disposed him to do the sorts of things he did that summer night, and to do comparable things in comparable circumstances at other times in his life. He seems to have believed in justice, in fairness, and he seems to have believed that it is morally right to assist those who cannot fend for themselves. If there had been no tacit assent to these "beliefs," it is difficult to account for his actions. Precisely in what ways these beliefs might function to "explain" his action is difficult to delineate. They seem to give a "dominant direction" to his activity (the term is taken from Ray Hart's book, cited above), and perhaps "in-formed" and "in-fluenced" (flowed into) his particular decisions in such a way that they justified what he did as well as directed it.

We might attempt to account for the sort of person one is by examining his dispositions. What the word disposition refers to precisely in this context of its usage again is vague; what I wish to suggest is a readiness to act in a particular way, without trying to "locate" that readiness in any particular human "faculty." My companion seems consistently to have had a readiness to act on behalf of persons to whom injustice was being done, or persons who were unable to defend their own interests. The ease and finesse with which he acted would lend support to a traditional doctrine of virtue; there was a "perfection" of an "operative power" so that his ordered actions seemed to flow from the sort of person he had become. We might introduce the term "attitude" here; whereas others who observed the cheating of the soldier remained indifferent, he had an attitude of concern for the soldier's well-being which disposed him to act at some inconvenience to himself on the soldier's behalf. He was a kind man; he was a just man. "Kind" and "just" as qualifiers of the sort of person he was suggest that he was disposed to act in certain ways. He was a courageous man; he was characterized by a readiness to do a courageous deed on behalf of others. Indeed, dispositions function in such a way that actions flow from them, are expressions of them, more than they are deeds done under a sense of obligation to certain moral principles or values. We have observed how he was not the sort of person who could state certain moral principles to which he adhered, or the sort of person who would consciously apply principles to the case in hand as the ordinary way of deciding what he should do. Rather, there was a readiness which predisposed him to decide to do certain things when the circumstances evoked it.

We have noted that the traditional concept of the moral virtues has sought to render an account of what we call dispositions here. Aristotle's account tells us that "moral virtue comes about as a result of habit" and not simply by nature. "Neither by nature, then, nor contrary to nature do the virtues arise in us; rather we are adapted by nature to receive them, and are made perfect by habit." We "learn by doing them." "We become just by doing just acts, temperate by doing temperate acts, brave by doing brave acts."[13] As a person acts in certain ways over a period of time, a certain quality is formed in his "powers" which disposes him to act on subsequent occasions in a similar way, or in such a way that the quality which has formed is expressed in those actions. Or, to put the matter in terms the modern Catholic theologian Romano Guardini uses, virtue denotes "that the motives, the powers, the actions and the being of man are gathered at any given time into a characteristic whole by a definitive moral value, an ethical dominant, so to speak."[14] Such a "characteristic whole" does not mean that on a new occasion one acts without deliberation about what one is to do; it does not mean that actions flow "naturally" in all circumstances. But it does suggest that one is disposed, one has a readiness, to act in particular ways.

If there are persons of virtue, so also are there persons of vice. As philosophers and theologians have long noted, the capacity to develop certain "habits" lies behind both. Perhaps with less sophistication this has been noted in common speech, when certain persons are judged to have "bad dispositions" and others to have "good dispositions." The point I wish to note is that we commonly use evaluative terms, not only with reference to particular acts, but also with reference to the readinesses of persons to act in particular ways. We make judgments about the moral worth of persons, as well as about their actions. What the point of reference ought to be for judging a person to be "good" or "bad" is a matter of philosophical dispute. We have already introduced certain Thomist language in our discussion; for St. Thomas, "a good habit is one which disposes to an act suitable to the agent's nature, while a bad habit is one which disposes to an act unsuitable to nature."[15] The normative elements come out of the further discussion about what man's true nature is. In a contemporary discussion, the philosopher Maurice Mandelbaum writes, with a view of moral life that is different from the classical Catholic one, "the morally good man is the man who is seen as being guided by an apprehension of objective demands in the situations which confront him."[16] He finds this generalization applicable both to the "conscientious person" who must wrestle to apprehend what is required and to "the man of spontaneous, frictionless virtue." It is clear that the morally bad person would not be guided by those objective demands. Thus what we wish to highlight here is that there are "readinesses" to act in particular ways, and these can be modified according to our judgments about the moral worth of them.

On the face of it, one might also look for the "causes" of consistency in certain dominant affections that a person has. There is a consistent order of the heart. It is difficult to make a claim that certain "emotions" characterize certain individuals, for emotions are evoked by particular occasions. While it is possible to say that a certain person is "prone to anger," different events might evoke his wrath. That certain sorts of occasions tend consistently to provoke wrath in a person is the observation which leads to opening the issue here. We have probably all observed persons who respond indignantly whenever they see something of which they disapprove. A moralistic Protestant might react in anger when he finds out that college students are living in coeducational dormitories, or that they can have liquor in their rooms; someone else might react in anger at the sight of students with long hair. Others might respond in deep indignation at the sight of children suffering from napalm burn or from severe malnutrition. My colleague seemed to react with restrained indignation when he observed injustice, not only in the New York bar, but on many occasions. Others might be "prone to joy" when they observe something being done that they judge to be right. Our responses to persons and events have dimensions of sensibility, of affections, of emotions, and these seem in part to "cause" our actions.

Feelings, emotions, affections, sensibilities—these are so uncertain in terms of their references that it might be well not to use the words. The analytical work being done on these terms and their usage is important,[17] and the looseness of their use here is acknowledged. A theologian partial to Puritanism might be excused if he refers for some insight to Jonathan Edward's *Religious Affections,* even though it is couched in the language of the eighteenth century. Edwards uses the term "affections" to refer to what exercises the will or inclinations; they move the person from a state of indifference to a state of caring, and to action. They are "vigorous" and "sensible," indeed he writes about how "the motion of the blood and animal spirits begins to be sensibly altered."[18] In spite of being a prisoner of the language of "faculties" of the self, Edwards's view of the affections indicates that they exercise not only the will to act but also the mind; they affect one's fundamental inclinations and one's desires.

One must constantly remember that what the terms we are using in this section seek to distinguish from each other are in experience intimately related. Kenny, for example, correctly observes that "beliefs, by themselves, do not lead to action;

whereas desires and emotions do."[19] The differences in the sorts of "believing" which I have suggested are in part differences in the affective states of the "believers." The readinesses to act that can be characterized would hardly find expression in deeds if they were not affectively moved and triggered. My point is a general one: there might well be in certain persons a tendency of the affections that makes their responses to moral situations somewhat predictable. Put most colloquially, we assume something like this when we say about an event, "That's going to make him very angry," or "That's going to please her." We might well expect that such continuity of affections as can be posited, on the basis of inferences from past actions of a person, is likely to generate a "motion of the blood and animal spirits" which leads to actions of a predictable sort in certain circumstances.

Earlier it was noted that when we speak of a person having character, we might simply be indicating a consistency in his purposes or his intentions. The language of purpose perhaps denotes to most readers an articulated or specified statement of an objective, or goal, and maximizes the intellective aspect. As classic Catholic thought and some contemporary philosophy remind us, one can speak of the intention of the will as well as the mind. I would hope that the reader does not divorce the intellect and the will in attending to this discussion. Humans are characterized by intentionality, by a basic orientation toward objects, goals, and so forth, and this intentionality has different degrees of generality and specificity.

Ray L. Hart, whose reflections on this matter are informed more by the phenomenological philosophers than by the British-American analytical ones, uses "intention" to "cover the self's complicity in the entertainment of incipient act," "to the 'direction' in which the self's foreground lies;" it is "the work of envisaging and enacting will."[20] A major burden of Hart's argument lies in making a case for the primacy of the will, though always in interaction with the activity of the intellect. He makes a useful distinction between "the intention of dominant direction" and "the intention of the specific project." The former is, in a sense, more general; it embraces "policy" with reference to specific acts and projects, but its object is not as precisely located.[21] With a greater stress on the functioning of the mind,

Stuart Hampshire also suggests something of the "directionality" of intentions. He writes, "In metaphorical terms, my intentions, like a torch throwing its light forward, illuminate resisting objects in their path."[22] With reference to the fundamental direction of one's life, intention provides an illumination of the way in which one desires to go, though it does not at this range of generality indicate all the specific projects one must fulfill in order to achieve one's purpose. But one also has intention with reference to more specific projects, with purposes which refer to particular actions in which one is to engage. At least one might expect that one's intentions to specific projects are harmonious with the dominant direction of one's larger intentions. Indeed, part of the practical life is exercising oneself with reference to particular projects in such a way as not to be dissonant with one's more basic direction of life. This is what marks a person of integrity.

Beliefs, dispositions, affections, and intentions are clearly interrelated in persons. It is not necessary here to go into differing accounts of the relationships. Rather we can point to a plausible interpretation of my associate at the bar. There was a "dominant direction" of his intentions which led our mutual friend to suggest that what he did that night was "just what you would have expected him to do." That dominant intention was toward the rectification of unfairness or injustices and toward acting for the well-being of those who could not care for themselves. His specific projects on that summer evening were "within" that dominant direction; his fundamental intention was like a torch into the darkness of the unknown and uncertain, shedding light on the obstacles that had to be overcome for him to fulfill that direction with reference to specific circumstances. It would be difficult to establish that the movement between the dominant intentions and the specific projects was one of conscious reasoning; he did not state his basic purpose and seek to apply its implications to the interactions between the soldier and the bartender, and those two and ourselves. It is probably fair to make a vaguer point, namely, that his dominant intentions "informed" his reflection and action as that was executed with reference to particular purposes in the sequence of events.

His dispositions, affections, and the beliefs we have inferred also were consistent with his dominant intention, and with his specific projects. His actions were episodic, they were specific with reference to circumstances; but there were at least tacit beliefs that were settled, nonepisodic in character. His readiness to act in certain ways was informed by and in accordance with those beliefs; even the affections which were provocable by particular events had a degree of predictability and also were in harmony with his beliefs and dispositions.

Before inquiring how religious faith and life might qualify the "sorts of persons" we become, it is prudent to return to a word I have consistently put in quotation marks, namely, "cause." That the use of this word is disputed has been indicated. I chose it to suggest that there are determinate aspects of persons which determine to some extent the sorts of things that they do. But it is clear that the effects of such "causes" are not simple; it is not like properly functioning pistons which in turn cause the drive shaft to move in an automobile. Having used the falsely simple term for purposes of short-hand convenience, I must now qualify it. Perhaps we ought to speak of these items as conditions. They are conditions of the person which persist, which are not whimsical and episodic, and which function in various ways with reference to action. They set certain general limits to human capacities for action; we cannot do, or be expected to do, what we do not have the capacities to do; that is, we cannot do those things whose conditions for doing are not present for us. In a sense they set limits not only of the possible but also of what we would normally do. We would not normally act in such a way as to violate some deeply held moral beliefs, though under some circumstances we might be coerced into so doing. More positively, these provide the conditions of possibilities for action, without determining precisely what action one will do. A moral belief, for example, that human physical life is of great value, is not in itself sufficient to determine what a physician ought to do in every possible circumstance affecting the practice of his profession. Perhaps if a belief were more absolute than that which was stated, namely, that human physical life is of "absolute" value, the enabling function of the belief would dictate a more specific directive in all circumstances. But many moral beliefs are not so absolute; rather they provide a basic justification for a range of action, and they give guidance to action without determining it absolutely. So also with dispositions, and affections, and at least with intentions to dominant directions; they are conditions which make possible and likely certain sorts of action without determining in themselves what action will be done.

The concept of the person as "agent" is widely used, I believe, as a way of accounting for the capacity to be to some degree self-determining within the conditions of his existence, and, in a sense, to draw those conditions and their consequences into actions which are "indeterminate" as well as determined, actions which while predictable are never fully predictable. Agency itself seems to refer to a capacity, or perhaps better to a bundle of capacities which enable a person to provide direction, governance, of his powers in such a way that what he does is his own doing. Agency is pointed to in the distinction between saying "x happened to me," and "I did x." "X happened to me" indicates passivity and not agency; "I did x" indicates that at least from the agent's point of view he could have done otherwise and that what he did was an exercise of his self-determination.

If this analysis of why one might say of a person, "That's just what you would have expected him to do" is reasonably intelligible, clear and persuasive (I have admitted that many refinements of each point are made in more technical literature), then we are prepared to move to the burden of this particular project. The question now is, in what ways might religious beliefs and religious life qualify these conditions which make for predictability, or for a measure of consistency in human action? More particularly, what difference might it make to the sort of person one becomes if one is conscientiously a Christian?

3 Christian Faith and the "Sort of Person" One Becomes

The exploration of the significance of the Christian religion and of Christian faith (the distinction is meant to indicate a higher degree of subjective commitment in the latter) for the sort of persons we become is a many faceted enterprise. One aspect of it would be a social-historical exploration of the significance of Christianity in the formation of certain widely held human and moral values in Western culture or in other cultures into which Christianity has been introduced. At one level this would require a comparative sociology of religion, such as that begun by Max Weber, in which the principal points of attention would be the ideational and institutional forms of religion, the moral and other outlooks of cultures, and the behavior of individual persons who are nurtured in the cultures. The knotty problems of historical explanation would have to be addressed, for while the sweeping generalization is patently true that Western culture is different from Indian culture, Moslem culture, or East Asian culture in part because the dominant religion in the West has been Christianity with its Judaic roots, the more difficult task is to substantiate with precision just how this came to be, what the connections are both between the religious beliefs and practices and the cultures and societies in which they occur and between these and the actions of individuals. But such a study of "Christianity and world history"[1] is beyond the scope of our project. Insofar as those vast issues do emerge in our discussion, the point of entry is through an understanding of what makes individual persons develop as they do.

Another aspect which will receive more attention in a subsequent chapter than it does here is the ways in which Christian faith might affect the sorts of persons we become through the uses of theological propositions or affirmations as premises in moral reflection and in moral argumentation. An example of this would be a process in which one would articulate certain statements about God, and would seek to draw inferences from these beliefs that would determine certain moral principles which in turn would provide both direction and justification for particular actions. Perhaps by engaging in such a conscious process one would eventually short-cut the conscious steps of reasoning, and the responses to particular actions would "flow from" the habituation of thinking. Here we are concerned to develop not so much an account of the uses of theological beliefs for the determination of particular actions as an account of the significance of *believing*, with its elements of trust and confidence, its elements of fidelity and loyalty, as much as its elements of "knowledge."

The preceding chapter dictated the pattern of this chapter. If the terms used there to develop an intelligible account of the sort of persons we become are persuasive, then the question is to what an extent, and in what ways, does being religious in that historical mode called Christian affect the sorts of persons we become. In addition to that, however, any theologically informed account of persons will have to consider the problems that Judaism and Christianity have denominated as sin, and thus this chapter concludes with a discussion of sin and transformation.

If one's genotype, one's "unconscious motives," and one's socio-cultural condition are in a sense "pre-moral," so it can be asserted that they are also "pre-religious," or at least "pre-faith." But to accept the first assertion prematurely with reference to the latter two would be to avoid some interesting and important issues for ethical reflection that are thrust upon us by the modern behavioral and social sciences.

It is patently clear that one's religious beliefs and faith have no impact upon one's genotype. For the sake of breadth of perspective, however, an observation is in order. Insofar as a religious community functions socially to determine bounds within which marriage is acceptable, not only is there a religious factor in mate-selection, but children born to such marriages are brought up in a distinctive religious culture. What one becomes as a person is conditioned by the interaction between one's genotype and, for example, a particular Christian religious environment. Insofar as a religious culture has an impact upon the sorts of personal aspirations and values that its members hold, it can have an impact upon the ways in which one's genetic potentialities are developed in the process of maturation. Since the form and significance of this interaction can be stated only in the most general terms, however, no precise interpretation is possible. Whatever becoming a "new creature" might mean in the discourse of Christian theology, it excludes the possibility of a new genotype. The obvious need not be labored, but if it is the case that certain forms of behavior, aggressiveness for example, which have serious moral consequences for others are dependent upon genetic factors, one cannot expect religious faith or morality fundamentally to alter that behavior. It is conceivable that it might condition the goals of such behavior as an agent conceives them, but not the aggressiveness itself.

The matter of "unconscious motives" or the "subconscious" is more complex and more puzzling. Do religious faith and religious experience in any significant way alter those aspects of personal life which, according to psychological evidence, are formed in early years of life and are beyond simple and easy access to rational control? Is it possible to claim that an experience of the reality of God, or trusting in God, transforms those wellsprings of human action which most of the Western world has come to believe are powerful in all persons? Or are they, in a strong sense, "pre-religious" and "pre-ethical?" If one were persuaded that the realm of religious and moral dimensions of experience were projections of the unconscious, totally determined by it, no claim for transformation could be made. If, however, one is persuaded that the interactions between religion and the unconscious are more complex, that religious faith and belief are not reducible to psychic needs, the answer is not so obvious. Certainly there is no consensus on the extent to which the exclamation of a religious person that he has "become a new person" carries with it a verifiable factual claim that his "unconscious" has been re-created or even transformed, that his basic personality structure has been significantly altered.

The issues are interesting and important if only because there are certain dispositions or affections which have been variously understood as Christian "virtues" or as "gifts of the Spirit" which are susceptible to an interpretation of their genesis which is psychoanalytic in character. For example, the Apostle Paul in his letter to the Galatians contrasts the "works of the flesh" with the "fruit of the Spirit." The fruit of the Spirit is "love, joy, peace, patience, kindness, goodness, faithfulness, gentleness, self-control" (Gal. 5:22–23, RSV). Of these terms, goodness is the most ambiguous; the others clearly refer to various qualities of persons for which certain psychological preconditions can be claimed to be necessary. The weight of psychoanalytical interpretation would rest on the side of claiming that certain persons, by virtue of powerful and profound experiences in the early stages of their lives do not have the preconditions to experience love, joy, peace, patience, and the like. The degree of overlap between this and other lists of the gifts of the Spirit and the virtues as they are discussed by Erik Erikson, in names if not in actual points of reference, is noteworthy. In his essay "Human Strength and the Cycle of Generations," Erikson discusses *"Hope, Will, Purpose,* and *Competence* as the rudiments of virtue developed in child-hood," *"Fidelity* as the adolescent virtue," and *"Love, Care,* and *Wisdom* as the central virtues of adulthood."[2] The "virtues" for Erikson refer to "ego strengths" rather than fruits of the Spirit, but one is provoked to reflect upon whether the Apostle's fruits do not also refer to strengths that members of the Christian community are to have. Although the particular list from the Epistles which I have quoted does not contain the word hope, in Romans 15:13 it is clearly a gift of the Spirit, and hope provides an interesting point for reflection both because Erikson discusses it and because it is currently enjoying some theological vogue.

Erikson makes a case for the view that the capacity to hope is dependent upon the experiences of a person's "pre-historic" era. He states that hope, "the most childlike of all ego-qualities, and the most dependent for its verification on the charity of fate," "relies for its beginnings on the new being's first encounter with *trustworthy maternal persons*, who respond to his need for *intake* and *contact* with warm and calming envelopment and provide food both pleasurable to ingest and easy to digest, and who prevent experience of the kind which may regularly bring too little too late."[3] There is a "verification" of hope in the experience of the infant before he learns to speak or remember words. While theologians might argue that Erikson's definition of hope is determined by the outlook of his discipline, I do not believe that some references to it would be left out of any Christian view. He says, *"Hope is the enduring belief in the attainability of fervent wishes, in spite of the dark urges and rages which mark the beginning of existence."*[4] At least formally, a Christian view of hope could affirm that it abides in spite of evidences that are at least in some respects contrary to it. Erikson recognizes that once hope is "established as a basic quality of experience," it "remains independent of the verifiability of 'hopes,' " that is, it endures without reference to particular objects of hope.

Our concern, however, is with what engenders and sustains hope in persons, as well as its significance for the moral life. If hope has to be verified by the "pre-historic" experiences of infants, and if the quality of hope, or the capacity to hope, cannot come into being apart from such experiences (a point not specifically made but perhaps implied by Erikson), is it meaningful to claim that hope is a gift of the Spirit, or that religious faith has the capacity to engender and sustain it? Can religious faith engender and sustain hope in persons who have had no experiential verification of a trustworthy person or of a trustworthy set of conditions? If hope is developed in the "pre-conscious," can one claim particular significance for religious faith in bringing it into being?

There are at least three approaches to answering these questions. One might, first, proceed to claim that the capacity to live the moral life with a disposition of hope exists only because one has had verifying experiences of the reliability of maternal care in infancy. Without such, one could not have the "established quality" (to use Erikson's term) that has a degree of independence from particular experiences. To say that hope is a gift of the Spirit, then, is simply to give a religious explanation for a psychologically based capacity. Or, more generously, it is to say that an experience of the reality of God will engender an outlook of hope only in those persons who have the necessary preconditions for it. Such a view is not to be dismissed with theological sophistication prematurely, for there are devoutly Christian persons who suffer long periods of the absence of hope, that is, of despair. One might, in a judgmental attitude, charge them with weakness of faith, or, more charitably, one might recognize that the "verifying experiences" of a religious basis of hope are at least temporarily not available, without impugning their religious faith.

A second approach could affirm that the hope of which Erikson writes has as its object "the attainability of fervent wishes" and that a religious hope is not a "fervent wish"; its object is God whose reality is beyond the vicissitudes of history and human relationships. Thus the hope of the Christian is something different not only in quality but in essence from the hope that the psychoanalyst describes. In sum, there is a radical disjuncture between the references of hope because each has a radically different basis and a radically different object. This approach would be dissatisfying in many respects, but mostly because it assumes that the religious dimensions of experience are somehow discontinuous with other dimensions of experience, the religious consciousness discontinuous with the "moral consciousness."

As a third alternative, one might claim that there is an interaction between the ground of hope that Erikson describes and Christian grounds of hope. From the psychoanalytical side, one might say that if a person has had no experience of a supportive relationship with a maternal figure, or with others, one's experience of the reality of God will not be such as to evoke hopefulness. Or, at least the evoking of hope is not so likely, or likely to be so significant as it will be with those who have had such "pre-historic" and "historic" experiences. From the religious side, one might say that the capacity to affirm that God is a firm and reliable object of hope ("Our hope is in God") depends upon having had some experiences of hope in other realms of life. Put in language used by William Lynch, if hope is "a sense of the possible," the capacity to respond to God as one who provides possibilities in human life depends in part on having experienced possibility (as against entrapment) in general human experience.[5] The awareness of God as a God of hope is affirmed by at least the memory of having had hope. But a process of interaction can well take place, that is, an experience of God as the provider of possibility for meaning and action might establish the quality of hope (to use Erikson's language again) in persons in such a way that particular experiences of hopelessness no longer count against it in the way that they previously did. There is a widening and deepening of the ground of hope through confidence that God is one in whom man can hope or, to make the point differently, that the ultimate source and power of life is one that creates and sustains possibility in human experience (and particularly moral areas of experience). This is not merely to find that a "more advanced set of hopes," as Erikson suggests, is involved in the process of maturation, but it is to have an experience of the reality of God's goodness and power which is a ground for lively and enduring hope even through the immediate sufferings of human life.

The question that I am unable to answer satisfactorily is whether one can claim that this "gift of the Spirit"—obviously rationalized here in order to render it more intelligible—really *transforms* one's "unconscious" or "subconscious" motives and outlook. The possibility that such can be the case is at least open, that is, that religious faith in and experience of God as one who offers newness (possibility) to all realms of experience can impregnate and penetrate one's personhood in such a way that those with good reasons not to have hope can become persons of pervasive and enduring hope.

I shall not pursue the engaging prospect of making a comparable analysis of Erikson's treatment of the "adolescent virtue" of "fidelity" and the "mature virtue" of "love." Suffice it to note that in each of these there are experiential bases in the process of human development and that the experience of the reality of God in religious life might have the same sort of transforming effect upon persons that is at least plausible with the "childlike" virtue of hope.

Claims for a "new creaturehood" which would involve a transformation of one's "subconscious" surely must be modest, and if made at all must be made with care. One's "subconscious" is to a considerable extent "pre-faith," and "pre-moral." As a college professor of mine delighted in pointing out, there is evidence in the New Testament that the Apostle Paul was aggressive before his conversion (his presence at the stoning of Stephen was evidence for this), and there is ample evidence that he was aggressive after his conversion. Thus a tendency to aggressive action was not transformed.

Another sort of claim, however, can be made. It is that an experience of the reality of God in one or more of its modes can well alter the purposes and directions which actions take, with full recognition that there are "pre-religious" and "pre-moral" factors involved in the determination of the purposes and of the actions which follow. The basic orientation of one's activity can be directed by experiences which have religious dimensions, and by the beliefs which inform and express the significance of those experiences. There can be reordering of the intentions, of those things which one values, and these reorderings can deeply affect the choices one makes without transforming the "sub-conscious" factors involved in the choices. One need not think of dramatic religious conversions in this regard; one can consider the ways in which through a development of religious life one's passive or aggressive tendencies are directed toward certain objects or ends in such a way that religious faith flows into and forms what one's preferences and actions are as a moral agent. For example, if part of the significance of faith through Jesus Christ is that a person seeks not his own interests but the good of others, as Paul admonished the Corinthian Christians to do (1 Cor. 10:24), differences in basic personality will make differences in how that admonition is fulfilled. Indeed, it has been fulfilled with scrupulous obedience in a compulsive way by some, it has been fulfilled in joyous abandon of the self for the sake of others by others; it has been a prime directive to aggressive social reform by some, it has led to a more passive inward self-denial in others. The religious meaning and the moral imperative flow into and form to some extent what a person does with his basic personality characteristics.[6] There is an accenting or coloring of what one is and does without a radical transformation of one's "subconscious."

The social and cultural conditioning which give shape to a moral agent are also "pre-moral" and "pre-faith" in the same way that one's "subconscious" is. Through socialization processes in particular religious communities, or in the family and other communities influenced by religion, persons internalize not only the language and other symbols but the values and outlooks of their religious cultures. Thus it is possible to make the claim that many persons who have no conscious commitment to the religious and moral values that have marked Western religious communities nonetheless view the world, and make moral choices, in such a way that those values are reflected in who they are and what they do. My colleague at the bar could be interpreted in this way. Defensively, and with excessive certitude, some persons might be prone to observe his actions and then claim that he could not have done what he did without having had a Christian nurture. If there is any evidence of such their claim might be made all the more vigorously. But that is surely an error. It is quite possible for persons to seek the well-being of others at the cost of their own interests without having been nurtured in particular religious communities. Other factors might be involved in the formation of the same moral outlook, including the possibility that something deeply universal in mankind is expressed in such actions.

To offer an account of the socialization process one would turn to the human sciences which have explored this more precisely: social psychology, sociology, and cultural anthropology. Comparative ethnologists have for years indicated that members of different societies have different "systems of values," and that there is sufficient consistency in practice within groups to warrant the assumption that the socialization of values within that culture and all its media of social interaction are to a great degree "causes" of that consistency. Recently James B. Nelson developed an analytical and prescriptive account of how this process does and ought to work within the Christian church. He uses concepts from "identity" theory in psychology, "reference group" theory in social psychology, and "role" theory in sociology to indicate how it is possible for a religious community to be a significant factor in the development of moral agents.[7] The socialization process is a "natural" one; it is not a process that one consciously chooses to undertake. It occurs whether one makes a commitment to the community or not, whether one engages in formed disciplines of religious socialization or not. One is reminded of nineteenth-century theologians who accounted for the experience of becoming Christian through the uses of the analogy of organism, Schleiermacher in Germany and Horace Bushnell in America for example. By participating in a community, understanding life in the light of its symbols, learning its values, sharing in its worship and language, what Bushnell called the "unconscious influence of grace" penetrated a person so that he could not remember a time when he was not "a Christian."

All of this process is a matter of "preconditioning" from a point of view which would claim that where there is no conscious choice to apprehend the symbols and values of a Christian community there is no serious Christian faith and morality. Indeed, in recent decades temporarily popular attacks have been made on "religion" in the name of its distinction from "faith." Religion, Barth and Bonhoeffer and their theological echoes reminded us, can itself be a form of sin, for one can rely upon its communal forms and their socialization processes without ever having a serious confrontation with a calling to a radical faith. At best the socialization is only a preparation to hear the gospel; socialization in morality is preparation to hear the direct command of God. At worst one has a theologically dubious cultural Christianity, or even a false security that by being socialized in a religious community one has faith. Faith, it is averred, comes by the grace of God and involves reliance upon his goodness and his command alone, rather than reliance upon what one is as a result of one's religious culture.

Whether or not one claims that socialization in a religious community, or in another community in which there are religious influences, is without theological significance and dignity is a clue to a basic theological stance that might be more implicit than explicit. It is also a clue to what a thinker is willing to include within the realms of experience relevant to ethics. In the theological sphere, one's claim suggests a position on the question of the relation of grace to nature, in this case not simply physical nature but the social and personal nature of experience. If one has a conviction about the social processes of life being grounded in the purposes and goodness of life's ultimate power and good, then these processes have at least the prospect of being channels of the divine beneficence toward man. If one is convinced that the purposes of God to fulfill and redeem life work through the mundane human experiences of living in communities, then socialization processes indeed have theological significance and dignity. On the other hand, if a radical disjuncture is drawn between socialization and the significant work of God's goodness toward man, so that the call to a religious and religiously moral life is a vocation which necessarily must be independent from, or even counter to, the socialization processes, then these processes have no theological dignity. If reliance to some degree upon what one has become through participating in a culture is per definition a reliance upon that which is less than God, and thus a form of unfaith, religion as a social phenomenon is sin. But another view is theologically defensible, namely, that becoming a person within the interactions of a particular society can be a process which mediates God's ordering and fulfilling intentions for human life.

In the more strictly limited sphere of ethics, the view has been taken that moral experience per definition begins with one's consciousness of one's capacities to be a self-determining agent, and thus what is significant to morality is restricted to those matters within one's sphere of accountability. But such a view can be expanded without losing the note of its importance, by recognizing that there are morally significant dimensions to experiences that are not entered into with specific moral intention. There is a socialization process through which certain values and even rankings of preferences for values become a part of the sort of person one is. To be sure, the more mature person examines what he has internalized, and affirms or rejects those values on the basis, it is hoped, of their moral sufficiency or adequacy. But does this mean that any action which is an expression of what one has become, a flowing with ease and pleasure from certain qualities that have been socioculturally developed, is outside the bounds of what is to be attended to in moral discourse? Great minds have argued that they are; Kant's arguments, for example, would make such actions "pre-moral," since they would not be determined by recognition of an obligation to obey the moral law. Our account of the emergence of the moral agent makes such a sharp distinction difficult to adhere to.

But to soften the distinction between what is faith and what is pre-faith, between what is moral and what is pre-moral, does not mean to assert that the sort of person one becomes is totally the result of being brought up in particular moral and religious communities. Surely there are the moments in which one affirms or rejects what one has become, if not in toto, at least in part. There are the occasions which prompt a reordering of the preferences and values that have become a part of one's character by virtue of socialization. There may be significant experiences in which one senses the Holy, the transcendent, that plant the seeds of transformation of what one is, that open a different frame of reference in the light of which one judges oneself, and that order one's intentions and activities. One might come to a conviction that certain moral and religious beliefs are of supreme importance, or are true, and thus redirect and reorder "natural" tendencies of character in the light of inferences drawn from them. The agent might find himself checking certain impulses to certain actions in the light of what he has come to believe he ought to be; he might redirect the capacities that he has accrued through social experience in the light of a religiously colored moral vision of life that he adopts.

How this works out can be seen from an example, namely, the Protestant religious communities of Mennonites. It would be imprudent to assume that all Mennonites are alike, that they all have the same moral and religious purposes, and that they are all morally commendable persons. But the external observer can hazard some generalizations about them and propose some ways in which to account for these. The willingness of the heirs of the morally rigoristic wing of the Reformation to live with relative simplicity so that they might be more generous in meeting the needs of suffering persons and communities in the world has been a mark of their communal existence. They have surely more consistently than most Christian communities sought to live out the Pauline injunction, "Let each of you look not only to his own interests, but also to the interests of others" (Phil. 2:4), or even the more demanding one, "Let no one seek his own good, but the good of his neighbor" (1 Cor. 10:24). Obedience to the cross, to the imperative of self-sacrificing love, without expectation of honor and reward from the world, has been a characteristic of their way of life from the beginning. This observation of a characteristic does not imply that there are no differences among Mennonites, or that there are none who have left their communities; it is a general, but plausible observation.

It would be difficult to account for this characteristic mark of Mennonite life without accounting for the processes of socialization which have gone on within the communities through the centuries. The sensibility to the suffering of others has been nourished in part by the recollection of the suffering of Christ in his obedience to God's will for self-giving love, and perhaps also by recollection of the sufferings of Mennonite martyrs. Individual members of the community have been shaped by its ethos of loving service to those in need; there has been a coherence between the professions of faith and the style of life and activities of the community. But surely there are also the conscious affirmations that Christian communities ought to be willing to give of themselves for the sake of others, and that individual members of the community ought to live in accordance with the biblically grounded, historically reinforced orderings of values. Socialization is there (and surely was more effective in a period and a culture in which there was less exposure to other cultural movements); the consequences of being shaped by participation in a community are morally and religiously commendable. But there is also a consciousness of being a Christian with a Mennonite cast of morality and life that is present among many; there is a commitment to living out what they have tended to become. Indeed, among some there is a vigorous defense of the beliefs and the moral imperatives derived from them as normative, not only for them, but for all Christian persons and communities.

The example, though not romantic, is too easy. The more difficult issue is that parallel to one raised in the discussion of Erik Erikson's view of hope, namely, whether a distinctively religious experience, or belief, can "transform" what one has been socialized to become, can alter that in a significant way. Again, I am thinking not only of the possibilities of dramatic "conversions" but also of less dramatic alterations in life. Do the claims of a Jonathan Edwards and other Puritan writers that the religious person has a "new sight" hold up to critical scrutiny? Or, in the end, does the "graced" person simply have another layer of socialization added to his life? Surely the testimonies of articulate participants in our contemporary counter-culture involve claims for radical transformation, for "seeing" life differently from how they saw it before. There is a rejection of the various values they were taught in the past—indeed, not merely which they were taught but by which they lived. There is a radical reordering of their preferences, and in some instances a very high priority given to "living for others" rather than for themselves. Seeing life differently requires that things be valued differently. If one is aware of this sort of transformation, it cannot but affect the way in which one understands the conversation between Jesus and Nicodemus reported in the Gospel of John. Jesus tells him, "Truly, truly, I say to you, unless one is born anew, he cannot see the Kingdom of God" (John 3:3). The metaphor of "new birth" carries with it the claim that one "sees" different things, or at least sees things differently. And, in seeing things differently, in seeing "the Kingdom of God," one values things differently. The emergence of a new religion itself seems to suggest that radical transformations of already socialized persons are possible. Thus the possibility of such transformations occurring cannot be ruled out.

But what is transformed? We have suggested that what one values can be altered, if not transformed, and that these objects of valuation in turn can alter the sorts of behavior, the purposes of actions, in which one engages. One's perspective can be altered, so that one understands his past differently (see Augustine's *Confessions* and other religious autobiographical litera-

ture), as well as the direction of his current and future life. The
Puritans' use of the notion of "new sight" is not far-fetched. It is
no doubt applicable not only to startling religious and moral
experiences of individuals but also to less dramatic participation
in the life of religious faith and faithful communities. In the
conviction that certain experiences of the Holy, certain beliefs
about God, are valid, persons and communities see (understand,
interpret) the significance of historical events, of man's relationship to nature, of themselves, to be different from what other
persons do. This is not to ignore that socialization is a part of this
process as well. For example, if a high respect for human physical
life is engendered by an experience of the body and of nature
around one being a gift of the goodness of God, seeing life that
way is nourished and reinforced by participating in a community
that revivifies the experience of God through liturgy and worship,
and through discourse about the value of physical life in the light
of its being a gift of God.

It would be foolish to claim too much for the distinctiveness
and transforming consequences of religious faith and experience
in regard to what men have become through participation in
particular societies and cultures. Only a cursory recollection of
the ways in which Christianity has been grafted onto the various
cultures to which it has spread, or an awareness that "black
Christianity" can be different from the Christianity of the white
middle class, is needed to keep one from claiming that the impact
of one's social origins is removed by an experience of the reality of
God in Christian terms. It is plausible to claim, however, not only
that religious communities tend to form persons with certain
preferences for values, including moral values, but also that a
conscious awareness of the reality of God, a living of a life of
faith, can alter the values that persons have come to hold. In some
instances surely there is a selection from among those things that
one has become: some are consistent with one's religious faith
and views of the world, and others are not. In some instances
there is a genuinely new perception of what moral purposes are
worthy of human adherence.

It has not been possible to omit consideration in the previous account of the matter which is most decisive, namely, the significance of religious beliefs for the sort of moral person one becomes. That our primary concern in this chapter is not with the uses of theological propositions in moral arguments has been noted. Indeed, the limitation of "ethics" to the processes of moral reasoning dictates a severe restriction on, and a consequent oversimplification of, what is involved in morality from a religious point of view. Thus here the concern is with "believing" as much as it is with "belief"; it is with an experiential and affective component of life as much as with ratiocination. More attention will be given to the latter in a later chapter.

In chapter 2 a case was made for the presence of a component of "believing" certain moral values to be worthy of adherence in the life and activities of my companion in New York. Various terms might be used to indicate what is involved: there is an "emotive" or affective aspect to believing particularly when one is dealing with conscientious religious and moral persons. There is an inclination of the will toward those values or principles which are "felt" to be preeminent in importance. Indeed, various sorts of experiences are themselves reinforcements, if not confirmations, of believing certain moral or religious outlooks to be true, or at least plausible.

Before one can set forth an account of the importance of believing in the realm of Christian morality, honesty requires that note be taken of an empirical observation which will surely render the whole enterprise of this section dubious if not mistaken to some readers. It is that not all persons whose experience has religious dimensions, who believe in the reality of God, whose perception and understanding of that experience and reality is couched in Christian terms, act in the same way. Equally conscientious and faithful persons engage in very different actions and are guided and judged at certain levels of practical moral reasoning by different principles. Two responses to this can be made. One is that the connections between religious believing and experience and moral activity are complex, not simple. To note first the level of moral reasoning, it is not possible to claim that certain theological affirmations entail in a strict logical fashion certain moral principles and values. I shall not be willing to concede everything on that count, however, for looser terms than entailment can be employed; the moral principles and values that inform and judge action ought to be consonant, coherent, and even consistent with one's fundamental beliefs. But since other matters are brought to bear in determining moral values and principles relative to action, religious beliefs are not the sole basis or the absolute determinant of values and principles.

Second, attention can be called to something previously noted, namely, that (to use a metaphor not previously introduced) religious belief and believing is refracted through the prism of what a person is becoming as the result of other experiences as well. Religious persons are not "clones" of Jesus Christ; they are not "carbon copies" of what is most distinctive about his being. Rather, their experiences of the reality of God, their believing in God, occur in and through the individual and social aspects of their beings, through their personal and cultural experiences. Religious faith and experience flow into and through what they are already becoming; indeed for those who are raised and nurtured in religious communities this process goes on from infancy in such a way that it is not possible to say that "there was a time when he was without religious components flowing into his life." Or, to take another term previously introduced, religious experience "in-forms" what one is becoming, not in the rather one-dimensional sense of providing data (information) to persons, but in the rather strong sense of being a part of the "formation" of what he is becoming; it in-forms him. Since what a person is becoming is also influenced and informed by many other factors in personal development, it is foolish to think that all conscientious religious persons will be "alike" and that all the actions which flow from their characters will be similar. The harder questions remain: how decisive is believing, and how decisive ought it to be? How decisive it is surely depends upon many factors. Some of them are related to the extent to which there are multiple exposures to different aspects of cultures in the socialization process. Others are related to the degree of conscientiousness of the person, to the extent to which he exercises his capacities of self-determination in the light of his religious beliefs and experiences. Others are related to how decisive an experience of the reality of God has been for an individual person, and surely the extent of decisiveness is related to a great many other factors. How decisive ought it to be? From the point of view of the Christian tradition, the answer is clear: religious believing and the experience of the reality of God ought to be the most decisive, most informing, most influencing beliefs and experiences in the lives of people.

Put rather formally, the question to be pondered is this: what consequences might there be for our moral dispositions, affections, and intentions from having an experience of the reality of God, from believing in God? and more particularly, of course, God as known in the Christian faith and tradition? If it is at least plausible to claim that one's beliefs, dispositions, affections, and intentions are important aspects of the determination of the sort of person one is, what is the impact of religious faith, experience, and belief on one's moral life?[8]

In Western religious traditions there has consistently been a close relationship between the experience of the reality of God and believing in God on the one hand, and the moral life (including the social morality) of religious people on the other hand. One finds, for example, in the "Holiness Code" of the Torah, in the book of Leviticus, that commands of God which are more distinctively religious in character are mixed with commands which are more distinctively moral in character. The "holiness" of God, while it is never reducible simply to moral qualities, always includes moral aspects. When the prophets bring the word of judgment to the community in the name of God, it is judgment both against "religious" idolatry and disloyalty on the one hand, and against immorality (including unjust deeds) on the other hand. Indeed, as Victor Furnish has recently demonstrated, in the New Testament one cannot understand the significance of what appears to be one moral commandment—to love your neighbor—without setting it in the context of the theologies of the particular writers of the books in which it is found.[9] Not only is there a generalized relationship of religious beliefs and morality, but there is a relationship between particular theological intentions on the part of particular authors and the aspects of moral life that they stress.[10]

If believing in God is a "construing belief" (the term is Julian N. Hartt's), if it is the basis for an interpretation of all aspects of experience, then what one has experienced about the reality of God, and what one has articulated about that reality will have a pervasive effect upon what one becomes as a person, and upon what one does. Hartt indicates in a very suggestive way that believing in God is the basis of "*an intention to relate all things in ways appropriate to their belonging to God.*"[11] I would suggest that it is not only the basis of an intention, though it is surely that; it is also the basis of certain readinesses to respond to others, and to events. Which intentions and dispositions are appropriate will be roughly correlated with the content of one's experience of God, with the articulations of who he is. The predicates one is willing to use with reference to the subject, God, make a difference to the moral lives of religiously persuaded and conscientious persons. If, for example, one believes that the ultimate power determining the course of the universe is bent on the destruction of all that the species *homo sapiens* values, one's moral outlook in many respects will differ from what it will be if one believes that the ultimate power is good and wills the good of what he has created. If one believes that God is just, but devoid of loving kindness, in moral experience one may become a coldly just person without elements of mercy and redemption. If one believes that what is speakable about God can be summed up in a description of him as an "indulgent Father," without elements of just ordering, one may have a morality which affirms that one's impulses are an adequate guide to conduct, and one need not repent of anything.

Later we shall explore the significance of certain aspects of the experience of God, as creator, as beneficent, as judge, as orderer, and as *telos,* or end. Here one example of a predicate will be used to indicate some of the connections between experience of God, believing in him, and the sorts of persons we become. That example is the affirmation that God is love. Several cautions need to be introduced in using this example. Love is not the only predicate used to adumbrate the meaning of God in human experience; God is power, he is just, and so forth. Thus while the generalization may be true that love has a primacy in the Christian understanding of God, and in Christian ethics, it is not the exclusive term to describe either God or Christian ethics. As H. Richard Niebuhr reminded readers about Jesus' experience of God, "Though God is love, love is not God for him," so we must remind ourselves that the terms are not reversible.[12] One could make love the exclusive predicate of God only by vastly ballooning its meaning.

How might one make intelligible the relations between believing that God is love and becoming a "loving person," as many Christians (and others) are, and more ought to be? What might the relations be between that belief and one's disposition, affections, intentions?

Indeed, one might wonder what would give rise to the belief that God is love. From one religious point of view, the answer to that is that he has revealed himself as a loving God in the scriptures. What that means will depend upon how "revealed... in the scriptures" is interpreted. If it means that there is a verbal revelation in a fundamentalistic sense, then one's belief that God is love is based upon the authority of the scriptures as the deposit of the "words" of God. But it might also be interpreted to mean that the people of Israel and the early Christian community experienced the reality of God in such a way that it was appropriate to think of him as a God who is love, or "whose loving-kindness endures forever." Surely an experiential component is present; without some indications in the lives of human communities that the reality of God is a loving reality, the notion would not have emerged in the records of those peoples' interactions with the power that they felt bearing down on them.[13] To state the matter in commonsense terms, a people would not have come to say "God is love" without having that possibility evoked and confirmed in their experiences. But the experience is always ambiguous: there is no statistical or indubitable verification in history or experience that the ultimate power is one of love. Indeed, as anguished souls like Job and philosophers through the ages have pointed out, it is difficult to live through suffering, tragedy, and moral evil and yet affirm that there is a sovereign power who is love. So one might say, belief that God is love is possible only as a "statement of faith"—and "faith" here would refer to a reliance which is not confirmed by reason and experience.

But before one takes that route, further explorations might be of value. We might consider the affirmation made succinctly by John E. Smith that against those who argue for an *immediate* experience of God, "every alleged experience of God would also be experience of something else at the same time." For Smith, this means, "The peculiar character of the reality of God is acknowledged together with the corresponding need for a medium of disclosure, and the medium is shown to be related in an intimate way to the reality it discloses."[14] Various sorts of human experiences might be the "media of disclosure" of the love of God, for God's love in experience is always an "experience of something else at the same time." Basic psychological insight might be drawn on here; in the vein of Erik Erikson, it can be claimed that one who has no experience of being loved cannot become a loving person. If one has no experience of being loved, or of a people being loved, it would be difficult to come to the point where one could affirm that God is love, that the power to whom man is responding is in part qualified by the adjective loving.

Thus the conditions under which one might come to such a belief are complex. It would be difficult to affirm that God is merciful (as part of his love) if one had never known mercy or forgiveness from those who loved one. Yet the experience of being forgiven by a child or by a wife is not of itself sufficient to warrant the affirmation that God is love. A sense of the transcendent, of the Holy, a sense of the power bearing down upon man, is required to make existentially and rationally plausible the move from the experience of being forgiven by others to the reality of God's forgiveness in the forgiveness of others. (In a similar way, to keep from becoming overly simple in speaking about the experience of the reality of God, a sense of the transcendent, the

Holy, is necessary to make plausible the move from the experience of being guilty for having harmed another to the need to be repentant before God, who is also a God of justice and of wrath.) Thus one might claim that there is a dialectic of experience and interpretation between human experiences of being loved by others and one's sense of the Holy whose love is mediated through the love of others.

Not many persons, however, begin that process *de novo*. The development of the Christian religion does not begin anew in each lifetime. One is born into and nourished in communities which provide interpretations of human experiences, and interpretations of the transcendent, the Holy, which is the object that evokes human response. To cite a personal experience, the church building that was my childhood ecclesiastical home had across its front a painting of the Gethsemane scene, and above it was printed, "Gud är Kärlek," God is love. The juxtaposition of the anguish and suffering of Gethsemane with the affirmation "God is love" made an indelible impression on my mind and spirit; in moments of the most severe uncertainty and doubt, of spiritual suffering, there is a recollection of a wider experience, a deeper experience, namely, of God's love. To have listened to preaching by a pastor, my father, whose favorite text was 1 John 4, and to have been nourished in human relationships in which the affirmation of God's love was embodied in his dispositions and responses, suggest how both historical and interpersonal dimensions enter into the formation of a construing belief. There was the historical and personal experience of the church, and of other persons, providing insight and interpretation, even when one's immediate circumstances might lead to an objection to belief. To be sure, there are moments of personal appropriation of the affirmation; there are moments of consent to its rightness; there are experiences of its "making sense" in one's own life. One appropriates an articulation of an experience, and the articulation assists one in designating the experience. The belief is in a sense an inference from the experience of the reality of the Holy; that it can become a construing belief, an orientation and direction within all of human experience, a basis for the interpretation of the significance of various aspects of life in the world, requires not merely a verbal confession but a "lived experience" of its reality.[15]

What then is the relationship between God's love and man's love? And man's dispositions, affections, and intentions?[16] We are not, as Luther and Anders Nygren have indicated, the "tubes" through which God's love flows out to others. To assert such is to deny that persons are agents with a degree of autonomy, and to deny that God's love is affected by its human "medium of disclosure." A readiness to love, to do what love requires (difficult as that is to decide) is evoked by experiences of being loved, by awareness of the reality of God's love disclosed in being forgiven, being sustained, being cared for by others. Love evokes, generally, a response of love; God's love evokes a response of love toward him and all that is in his care. But surely the growth of a "loving disposition" is not only the result of momentary responses to being loved. It is the result of living out the reality of love, determining within one's capacities to do "habitually" what is loving. As many authors have pointed out, most recently Victor Furnish, in both the ancient Torah and in the teachings of Jesus love is *commanded*, hard as that is for us to grasp in an age attuned to the conventional wisdom of certain psychologies and styles of life. To be in the process of becoming a loving person is not simply a matter of the spontaneity of loving emotions but a determination of the intellect and of the attitude of the will. Fortunately, to obey the command to love is not always a matter of having to resist one's inclinations; there is a degree of correspondence between the reality of the love of God, the natural and developed capacities of the human person, and the obligation to become the sort of person that is consistent with the construing belief that God is love.

What I have stated is, in a sense, a restatement of the idea of the virtues as this has been developed in Catholic moral theology. Primal human experiences of love, arising out of preconscious "needs" or "ends" of man, lead one to be responsive to the experience and insight that the ultimate power is a loving power. But the capacity to give some determination to an outlook toward the world, to the directionality of one's intellect and will, means that persons can become agents of love, indeed of God's love. The development of a "quality" of one's powers to act so that there is a readiness, a disposition, to act in love is not merely the result of random experiences. Rather, there is a process of habituation, of governance of one's attitudes and actions, which forms and nourishes one's capacities.[17] To be sure, that process is not a uniform one in all religious moral persons. There are those whose acts flow with "ease, consistency, and pleasure" from loving dispositions; St. Francis and many persons unknown to history have been admired because of the wholeness of love that has dominated their lives. There are others whose capacities of self-determination must be exercised with consciousness of purpose, who must be reminded of a commandment, "Thou shalt love." Many must wrestle with the problem of what love requires under ambiguous conditions, and often there is no clear answer. (To remember that love is not the sole "virtue," the only command, is once again important. To have a readiness to love, to do what love requires, is not of itself a sufficient basis for conscientious moral action.) God's love is mediated through human agents, and agents differ in their experiences and capacities, the stages of their personal development. Thus, in a sense, one must make limited claims relative to the readiness to act in love: it is both enabled by the experience of the love of God and commanded by his purposes for men and their communities.

Contemporary usage in common speech suggests that an affectionate person is a loving person; that loving affections are the only true "affections." Such, however, is a mistake. Yet the mistake is interesting for our purposes, for it suggests that in common sense observation and discourse there is an assumption of a persistence of certain affective qualities in persons, or at least that under certain conditions these affections will be predictably evoked. One would hardly wish to claim that all conscientious Christians are, or even ought to be, "affectionate" persons, since the factors which make such a qualification possible are by no means exclusively dependent on a religious life. But there is a rough coherence between the experience of God as in part, even in Calvin's theology, an "indulgent father" and persistence in the affective capacity to make loving responses to others. Among the "religious affections" is the loving affection, the emotive readiness to be forgiving seventy times seven times, to go the second mile, to seek the vulnerability of loving responses, to engage in acts of costly service to other persons, and for their sakes to participate in corporate actions for justice and for peace.

The connections between God's lovingness and loving affections, while not easy to develop, perhaps in the Christian tradition are mediated principally through the narratives of the gospel accounts of Jesus. Whether such was the intent of the gospel writers or not, it is clear that the recorded and interpreted memories of the early Christian community portray Jesus not merely as "medium of disclosure" of God's love but as a person whose affective and active responses to others were loving in their qualities.[18] Indeed, if one is asked to indicate what he means by loving affections responsive to God's love, one is more likely to tell a story than to render a philosophical account. For persons nurtured in the biblical narratives, some gospel accounts of Jesus' deeds, as well as of his teachings, come to mind. In the face of insistence upon retributive justice for a woman caught in adultery, comes the disarming response, "Let him who is without sin cast the first stone." In the face of the calculations of prudence, or even of justice, comes a saying that one ought to give both one's cloak and one's coat. Such responses appear to be grounds for claiming that not only did Jesus follow the command to love, not only was he disposed to do acts of love, but there was an affective sensibility which made him identify with the needy, the immoral person, the victim of prejudice. There was a coherence between his affections and God's love for man, between his affections and the belief that it is fitting to speak of the ultimate power bearing down on man as having the quality of love.

Narratives, biographies, and imaginative literature will continue to function to transmit insight into the ways of life that are consonant with believing in a loving God. The transit between the object of faith and love and hope on the one hand, and faithful, loving, and hoping persons on the other occurs through the media which portray in suggestive detail and specificity what a loving manner of life is, what affections are fitting in relation to a religious belief. The loving affections are evoked more powerfully by the narrative and the parable than by more general commands.

As we have noted, however, love is commanded in the Jewish and Christian scriptures. God's love not only enables persons to become loving in their individual ways; the God whose steadfast love endures forever lays a duty on persons to be loving, and to do what love requires. All men, and most certainly those who profess that God is loving, *ought* to love. This can be developed in terms of the intentionality which ought to orient them toward the events and persons in their world, indeed toward nature as well.

The matter of an intention to love can be pursued in various dimensions. In one usage, perhaps the most common sense one, the intent to love, or to do the loving act, refers to a sort of mental act, to a conscious purpose that one has. In this usage both the agent and the observer often find themselves judging the discrepancy between their intention (purpose) and their performance. In religious moral language, the justification for this has been developed in alternate ways. First, there is a command of God to love one's neighbor as oneself. The agent is to be obedient to the command, and thus it is his purpose to fulfill his duty as an obedient person. He consciously seeks to live according to the divine command in his exercises of power in relation to persons and events. Thus he and others evaluate his actions according to their consistency with his intentions; both the means used and the consequences are often so judged. For example, there is a history of discussion about whether coercion or violence can be used by those who intend to do loving actions, even though the consequences are for the "well-being" of others. Can one obey God's command to love, can one have that as his dominant and specific purpose, and bear arms against an enemy, even for the sake of justice? Also, the consequences are judged relative to the intention to love. For example, John Noonan indicates that one basis for the traditional Christian stand against abortion is that an intention of Christian morality is to love, and it is inconsistent with this purpose to take defenseless fetal life.[19] Discrepancy between the intent to obey God's command to love and the means used and consequences occurring leads to the obvious charge of hypocrisy.

A second justification refers less to a pattern of command and obedience, and more to a pattern of the "imitation of God," a reason for acting morally which receives more extensive treatment subsequently. Here the morphology is something like this: God's purposes are loving; indeed, God's deeds are, among other things, loving deeds. In gratitude for God's acts of love, the religious person intends to act lovingly, that is, consonant with and in imitation of God's actions. Thus it is his conscious intention (purpose) to act in a loving way toward others. The practical moral question then is: What means and ends of action are in accord with God's will—that is, with his purposes and his actions? The process of evaluation that takes place here is the same as that in the command, duty, and obedience model.

But there is another usage of intention to love, and of terms related to intention, which also has a long history in the Christian community. Put simply, it affirms that there is a basic love or, to use our term, intention inherent in the being of man which is directed toward its proper end, the good. The ultimate good is God; thus there is a natural tendency toward God. The early Christian and Catholic traditions have developed this into an ethic of the love of God, or the "vision of God."[20] In one's proper orientation of one's being, that is in one's love for God, one is rightly oriented toward moral ends. Tending toward God leads to an intention of one's whole being toward the world which issues in actions in accord both of God's will in creation and man's basic and proper nature. The agent's conscious purpose is to love in accordance with the fundamental intentionality of his being.

Surely St. Augustine was a principal formulator and source for this tradition.[21] In the *Confessions*, he speaks metaphorically about the weight (*pondus*) of a body which makes it move or strive toward its proper place. "Fire tends upward, a stone downward. They are urged by their own weight, they seek their own places.... When out of their order, they are restless; restored to order, they are at rest. My weight, is my love; thereby am I borne, whithersoever I am borne."[22] This seems to suggest that there is an intention or orientation of one's whole being toward its proper end; for Augustine this was God, and in him the restlessness of hearts would find their peace. It is the object of love that determines whether the intention of one's being is well directed or not. Later, in *The City of God,* in a famous passage, Augustine wrote, "The right will is, therefore, well-directed love, and the wrong will is ill-directed love."[23] The right will is an intention of the will toward its proper end. The more distinctively religious end—God—is not, however, without its moral significance. In another well-known section of *The City of God,* book 19, he works this relation out with reference to the peace of the "heavenly city" and the pursuit of peace in the "earthly city." There is an analogy between the two; peace is "the tranquility of order." "Peace between man and God is the well-ordered obedience of faith to eternal law. Peace between man and man is well-ordered concord.... Order is the distribution which allots things equal and unequal, each to its own place."[24]

I wish neither to commend nor criticize here the static tendencies of Augustine's notions of peace and order, related as they are to his view of God. Rather, a more formal point is in order, namely, that when one's being is rightly tending toward or intending God, when one's love is rightly directed, there will also be a right intention and direction of specific projects. Thus what one is by virtue of God's creation, a creation weighted toward the good, can become realized to some extent in the moral life as one has the right objects of love. Indeed, it is not too much to say that one's loves govern one's intentions, and that the moral life consists in the right ordering and directing of one's loves.

The religious life of worship and of prayer helps to give direction toward the right ends. Put in a theological framework, the work of God's love (grace) both in his creative and in his redemptive activity gives direction to man's nature; it moves the "weight" of men so that they are properly oriented in their beings toward the Good (both the moral and the extra-moral Good). This is a "conversionist" or "transformationist" claim of the most fundamental sort.[25] It does not claim a perfection, moral or otherwise, of one's life as the result of the experience of the reality of God, but it does claim a new and different "intending," a redirecting of human action toward God, and toward others. Perhaps Julian Hartt's phrase catches the significance of this. Believing in God, he says, is the basis of "an intention to relate all things in ways appropriate to their belonging to God." This intention is a matter both of conscious purpose relative to specific actions and of the persisting direction and orientation of one's being and doing. One might translate Hartt into Augustine's idiom: The experiencing of the reality of God, believing in God, orients one's love, one's weight (*pondus*), toward loving all things in ways appropriate to their being loved by God.

The focus on love here, to remind the reader again, is not made as a substantive point that would collapse all things into love, that would make love the be-all and end-all (in weightier senses than colloquial usage of these terms suggests) of the Christian life and action. Rather, love is selected as an example of one way in which the claims of religious life and experience have consequences for moral intentions.

There is yet another key document in Christian literature to be attended to in trying to make intelligible the claims that believing in God as a loving God has consequences for the moral life of the Christian community, and it also concentrates on love. The document is 1 John 4:7–5:12. In one way or another it seems to make all the claims we have attempted to analyze in our discussion of love.

The setting of the people to whom this letter was written was one in which Christian faith had to be interpreted against Gnosticism and its claims. Thus there is a polemical intention, as is clear in the writer's warning that the Christians are to test the spirits to see whether they are of God. For our use, however, of greatest interest is the claim of relations between God's love, man's reasons for loving, man's loving, and the command to love. Since the writer is drawing on themes he has previously introduced, and since his purpose in the passage is not the same as our analytical one, our discussion of 1 John 4:7–5:12 requires that we alter the sequence of the texts.

There is a range of statements, each of which makes a special point in the total account of the relation of God, his being and his love, to men, and to what men ought to be and to do. One is a straightforward assertion, "God is love" (4:8b and 4:16b). The author finds it fitting to denominate the predicate of God as love. But this does not function as the major premise of a practical syllogism in the context of the letter. There are accounts of the sorts of experiences which make the assertion plausible. The person who loves "knows God," indeed is "born of God" (4:7b). There are reasons given for believing that God is love, for he has made his love "manifest" to the Christian community in "that God sent his only Son into the world that we might live through him" (4:9). Indeed, it is not that we first loved God, but "that he loved us"(4:10). But the reasons are the reasons of the heart: there is a "personal" relation between man's loving and the presence of God. "If we love one another God abides in us and his love is perfected in us" (4:12b). "God is love, and he who abides in love abides in God, and God abides in him"(4:16). One cannot read the sentence "We love, because he first loved us" merely as a rational justification for our loving; the "because" suggests that God's love empowers our loving. Thus far, it is clear that a relationship of love between God and man, and relations of love between man and man are the basis of the claim that God is love, that man "knows" God by loving, that in man's loving he "abides" in God; and that there is a "manifestation" of God's love in his actions in "sending" his Son.

But the writer also states certain imperatives, as well as a quality of being, that are consequences of the loving relationship between man and God. He makes the great claim that "there is no fear in love, but perfect love casts out fear. For fear has to do with punishment, and he who fears is not perfected in love" (4:18). Obviously perfected love does not occur with frequency; the section has its share of admonitions as well. "*Let us* love one another, *for* love is of God"(4:7). The imitation of God theme is present. "*If* God so loved us, we also *ought* to love one another" (4:11). A revision of the love command is set in the context of this passage: "And this commandment we have from him, that he who loves God *should* love his brother also" (4:21). Indeed a proper love for God is shown by keeping his commandments (5:3). Finally there is a "behavioral test." "If anyone says, 'I love God,' and hates his brother, he is a liar, for he who does not love his brother whom he has seen, cannot love God whom he has not seen" (4:20).

It is not grossly unfair, I believe, to seek to relate this passage to our ongoing analysis. The writer is suggesting that there is an experience of the reality of God as loving, which is grounded both in man's loving and in believing that God sent his Son as an act of his love. This experience and this believing are warrants to claim that God is love. From this experience and believing certain consequences follow. Persons are enabled and ought to be loving persons. Also, an intention toward others is demanded: Christians *ought* to love one another, they *should* love their brothers. Both an enabling and a requiring are present relative to what Christians ought to be and to do.

Even in literature that claims a great deal in the indicative mood for the consequences of the experience of the reality of God, and for the consequences of religious believing, there exists an imperative mood as well. There are both claims of enabling faithful people to become a certain sort of persons, and there are requirements about the sort of persons they ought to become. Christian ethics is not merely a description of how people live in the Kingdom of God, as Schleiermacher suggested.[26] It is also normative; there are claims about the sorts of persons, their intentions and dispositions, that are consonant with and required of members of the Christian community.

There are several bases for this normative aspect. Surely the principal one in the Christian and Jewish traditions, as I indicated earlier, is that God's will is a moral will, that there is a "law" of God. And surely another is that simply the finite human character of the Christian community requires that there be some instruction in the forms of conduct fitting their faith and life. Even the most "sanctified" person needs to be "goaded," as Calvin pointed out.

But there is another basis pertinent to our present discussion, namely, that the "sort of person" any human becomes is qualified by his condition as sinner. Throughout the history of Christian communal life there have surely been many persons who, if asked what sort of persons they were, would respond, "I am a sinner." This confession refers not only to the judgment that one's moral actions have "missed the mark," have violated the moral law to which the community owes obedience. It also refers to a quality of one's person, to a pervasive human condition.

Immoral acts flow from the sort of person one is, as well as do moral acts.

This is not the place to rehearse the interpretations of "sin," to survey various accounts of the genesis of this condition and its forms of disloyalty, unfaith, sloth, pride, and so on. Rather, one needs only to note that, in any interpretation of the "sort of persons" Christians are becoming, account must be taken of the fault in human life, as well as of its commendable prospects and achievements. Accounts so taken have been weighted by various theologians in various ways, depending upon their theological and other preferences. If, for example, the moral life is viewed primarily in terms of obedience to written commands, the account of sin will focus on the term disobedience. If it is viewed primarily in terms of being and acting in accordance with one's "true" nature that inclines toward the good, the account will focus on what causes persons to violate that inclination. If moral life is viewed as the loving expression of one's lively trust in God, the account of sin will focus on man's lack of trust and its "fruits." Those interpreters who have weighted their interpretations of sin toward moral terms such as disobedience to God's law have always also developed views of the "roots" of that disobedience. Those interpreters whose weight is on the "root" sin of unfaith have always also developed views of the immoral "fruits" that are consequent upon unfaith. Thus, in all serious theological views of morality, there is need for admonition, for normative ethical prescription of the sorts of persons Christians ought to become, and the sorts of actions they ought to take.

Surely, then, one basis of the limitations that have to be made on claims for the significance for moral personhood, the experience of the reality of God, and believing in God rests in this religious interpretation of the human condition. Man's dispositions, affections, and intentions are biased toward improper self-interest; man is curved in upon himself. This he never overcomes in a human perfection of his moral capacities; the problem is not merely that "grace" has to work in and through the particular and limited capacities of what individual persons are becoming as a result of their genetic endowments, their "prehistoric" relations with parents, and their being bound by their cultures. The problem is a disorientation of their basic direction, and this also must be overcome. There is a persistence in experience of that disorientation, and thus limited claims are necessary.

That my companion at the bar was a virtuous man, few persons would disagree. That he was a Christian virtuous man was not the case. His persistent moral characteristics were not nourished by participation in the Christian church; he did not believe that God is loving, or that he is the ground of hope; he had no sense of a power standing over against him to which he was responding and responsible. His life was surely nourished by his participation in communities; he had moral beliefs in which he profoundly believed; he was responsive to persons and to events. Perhaps he would have suggested with a touch of quiet cynicism that some persons might need the props of religion to bolster their characters, but for him it was not necessary. With that I could not disagree, but that would be beside the point of this chapter. That persons can have praiseworthy moral characters without being religious or, particularly, Christian, cannot be gainsaid. That some persons are consciously religious to prop the weakness of their moral characters is equally evident. I could not argue that he would have been a "better" moral person if he had been a Christian; evidence could be readily gathered that many of us who bear some of the marks of being Christian are morally "worse" than he. What I have attempted to indicate is that if one experiences the reality of God, particularly in the context of Christian history and life, there are or ought to be consequences for the sort of person one becomes morally. There is no ground to condemn my friend morally because he was not a Christian, nor can I find any ground to condemn him "religiously" because of that. There is ground, however, for questioning the integrity and wholeness of one's own life if one purports to be Christian but does not bear some marks in one's moral character of that living and believing.

Much that many Christians like to claim has been omitted from this chapter. There is, for example, no ringing account of the freedom of the Christian here. Some of what has been omitted here will be developed in the next chapter, in which I will interpret some of the reasons for being moral that are religious in character, and the ways in which those reasons affect the person and his actions.

4 Christian Faith and the Reasons of Mind and Heart for Being Moral

Reflection on the moral dimensions of experience can move in various directions, as we saw in the first chapter. The previous chapter sought to offer an intelligible answer to the question, "How does the Christian experience of the reality of God, and Christian believing in God, affect the sort of moral agent one becomes?" In this chapter our concern is the question, "Why be moral?" The philosophical and theological literature on this question is rather extensive, and it is not our purpose to survey and assess it. Rather, we are concerned to give a constructive interpretation of the major religious reasons of mind and heart for engaging in a life of moral seriousness.

It is clear that not all the reasons for being moral, even in a religious community, are distinctively religious; and thus surely it is the case that many conscientious moral persons offer no religious answers to the question that concerns us here. Whether in the end decision is king in answering the question, even for the most rational man, is an open and debated issue. Perhaps each self-critical person can give reasons for his moral seriousness, but that they would be persuasive to all rational persons, and thus provide a universally acceptable answer, is not likely to be the case.

My colleague at the bar on Lexington Avenue, as I have described him, was not given to justifications for his moral activities, but we might simulate a conversation with him, a conversation he would have regarded as barren, sophistic, and sophomoric. "Friend, why did you object to the soldier's being cheated at the bar?"

"Well, if you insist on silly academic questions, the bartender was dishonest, the transaction was dishonest, and I believe in honesty."

"Now, what makes you believe in honesty? Why is honesty important?"

"That seems obvious enough, but since you insist on being told the obvious, I will tell you! Because human society just cannot function well if persons are dishonest with each other. Human conversation and activity cannot take place smoothly and efficiently if we cannot presume that people are fair and truthful. Indeed, what would happen to the fabric of society if we could not rely on each other to tell the truth, to give us correct change?"

"But, my friend, I notice that you suspected the bartender of being dishonest. You must have suspected that he might give incorrect change, or else you wouldn't have watched the transaction so closely. And you doubted whether the cabbie we got on the street would be honest. You certainly showed him that you were not sure you could trust him."

"Well, I've been around, and one has to be realistic. You've got to check on these things, not only for the sake of the person who might be wronged, but to keep the fragile fabric of society together."

"What makes you care about the fabric of society? Why does that concern you?"

"My God, you academics either play games, or are blind! Because persons can't have any realization of their own lives if there is not some measure of order, reliability, and harmony in their relations with others. How would you ever be free and productive if you had to worry like a paranoid all the time about whether you will be cheated or lied to?"

"Fair enough, I guess, but tell me why you are concerned that we realize ourselves? Why are you concerned about that?"

"Do I really have to tell you? Well, because we just are, that's all. That's the way we are."

If I could push my colleague no farther, we might say that he had given us his justification for morality. Why be moral? Because it is in the interests of all individuals who are fundamentally interested in self-realization to be moral. We might have succeeded in getting a believer in God to take this conversation a step further. He might have said, "We are concerned to realize ourselves because God created humans to be that sort of creature." Clearly one would want to ask, "Why did God create men that way and not some other way?" While a learned theologian might offer an extensive answer to that question, many persons would simply say, "I don't know. Who am I to know God's reasons? That's just the way he created the human race." And thus we would have a reason for being moral.

Clearly there are nonreligious reasons for being moral. It would be foolish to argue that if one desired to be moral, one must be religious, unless we take "being religious" in functional sense and claim that whatever reasons or symbols or concerns one appeals to as final in this process of regress are by definition "religious." But our interests are in religion in somewhat more precise historical and experiential senses. We are keeping a historical tradition in view, the Christian one, and also maintaining that the experience of the reality of God is that of "a power bearing down on one."

Many persons in our culture were brought up to believe that they could not be moral without being religious, and, indeed, perhaps one reason for the decline of commitment to Christianity and Judaism on the part of many persons is that they have found out that such a belief is mistaken. Surely a lingering thread that still pulls parents of small children to church schools on Sundays is the aspiration that learning about God, about Jesus, and about the Bible will make the youngsters better in a moral sense. Indeed, there are those whose primary interest in religion is that it props up morality. The props take different forms. Some believe that persons will not be moral without the threat of punishment, and so God the awesome Judge walks on the stage to cajole men and to threaten them with eternal damnation for their evil thoughts and deeds. Others believe that without a sense of a personal relation with the ultimate power and giver of life, persons will not have the sort of basic respect for life which grounds a sense of responsiblitiy for one's self, for other persons, for society, and for nature. Further elaboration of the forms of religious props for morality is not necessary. It is clear that one could list many evidences to the contrary of these beliefs. My colleague at the bar, a moral virtuoso, was in no recognizable sense a religious man, yet he was highly commendable from a moral point of view.

Our approach is this: if one is a religious person, what reasons of mind and heart does one have for being morally conscientious. This has to be distinguished from another sort of inquiry, namely, that into the "theological foundations," or "theological presuppositions" of morality. We have shown that a person does not have to be religious in order to be moral. That is a different issue from the one we wish to exclude now, namely, whether there are metaphysical assumptions, ontological assumptions in morality which are in the end "theological" assumptions. That inquiry has a long history and is worthy of exploration in philosophical theology. The inquiry has led in a number of directions. For some, there is evidence of an order, a direction, and a purpose in human life and history to which persons and societies must conform. If this order, direction, and purpose is violated, human life in its richest dimensions, perhaps even the survival of the human race, is in peril. This order and direction is God, or at least is the immanence of God in creation. For others the positing of God is necessary to guarantee that those who obey the moral law shall be rewarded in the future life even if they suffer for righteousness' sake in their present lives. Thus one has, in the manner of Kant, a resolution of the problem of evil. In each of these two examples, one would be engaged in a moral argument for the existence of God.[1]

To rule out of our inquiry the moral justifications for religious life, and for the existence of God, is not to deny that such justifications have not been, and are not, important for many persons. Persons are led or even driven to belief in a loving, merciful, and forgiving God out of deeply felt needs for release from a profound sense of guilt for moral wrongs they have done. Persons are scrupulously conscientious in their moral actions out of fear of divine punishment. Persons do come to believe in an ultimate power and order on the basis of inferences drawn from the necessary conditions for morality. It is the case, however, that unless persons are religious for other than moral reasons alone, "functional equivalents" for God can be found to meet these spiritual and intellectual needs. Persons can get absolution for their guilt from a therapeutic community rather than God; they can be scrupulously moral out of a commitment to certain principles as being moral absolutes rather than out of fear of God's wrath. A secular ontology can serve as well as God to satisfy the quest for the necessary conditions for morality.

Thus again, our concern is to interpret the reasons that religious persons and communities give for being moral. We will be alert to possibilities that these reasons might also affect the way in which they live their moral lives. This point is of interest because there are philosophers who argue that there is no intrinsic relation between one's metaphysical, theological, or other justifications for morality itself, and the morality that is thereby justified.[2]

In the first chapter I interpreted the moral dimension of experience as occurring in relationships, in interactions between persons, and between persons and events and institutional powers. The religious person and community, in its experiencing of the reality of God and believing in God, has another dimension, or horizon, in moral life. In a sense, the relations involved in human moral activity are more "extensive" than appears; the interactions go beyond those we immediately perceive to be significant in the determination of our actions. In religious language, persons are not only related to other humans, to events, and to institutions but are related to God in and through these other relations. These interactions are also with the Holy power, the moral will which is God. To use religious language, human experience is possible because there is a power and purpose that brings life into being, that gives it form and direction; human actions are related to that power and purpose willy-nilly. A normative prescription is derived from this: human action ought to be responsive to and governed by that power and purpose of life.

The experience of the reality of God is mediated through a community and its traditions. These traditions are themselves records—in narratives, poetry, cultic forms, interpretations of historical events, theological ideas, laws, and other forms—of the experiences of previous generations and of the significance of these experiences in the light of ideas and symbols of God that have been developed. The notion of God as one who gives moral commands, for example, seems to have emerged out of an experience of an ultimate power to whom persons are obligated; this power has a moral will. The language of commands entails a commander; people perceived themselves in a social and political role in which God had authority over them similar to the authority of their temporal rulers. To articulate their experience of ultimate obligation to God they used the symbol of a commander; to articulate what they were obliged to obey they used the language of commands, or laws. The reason for being moral was that God commands it. This "made sense" of their experience of an ultimate power whose will was a moral will; their symbolization of their experience came in part from their experience in a human community.

The reasons for being moral within the biblically informed communities are several, even in their theological articulation and symbolization. Several dimensions of the community's experience of God were seen to bear on the requirement of morality. Systematic theologians desire to find a principle by which to provide a unitary theme, or around which to organize symbols in a coherent way, but the more ordinary language of the scriptures is very pluralistic. To note the variety is not to denigrate the intellectual value of providing thematic coherence as a part of the theological task. It is, however, to suggest that the variety of languages used to articulate experience issue in reasons for being moral that can be differentiated from each other.

After illustrating this variety, an effort to order it will be made. To show the variety, however, will be to suggest that the ordering generalizations lose some of the richness of more concrete references.

God was experienced as the *creator*; from his power and will have come all that is. What is, including persons and their relations to each other, is dependent upon God. The *dependence* of the finite created life on the superior power of the Creator is a condition that requires the ordering of the created forms of life in correspondence with their Creator's will. Morality is part of that requirement.

God was experienced as having *led his people* out of bondage, and in so doing he made a covenant with them. Their freedom enables them to fulfill their vocation under him; they also are obliged to *abide by the terms of the covenant* that has been made. These terms are stipulated in the Torah, in the law. The people must be moral because of their covenant, their agreement with God.

God was experienced as the *sovereign Lord*; by virtue of his sovereignty he has a *right to command,* for "I am the Lord." Those over whom he is Lord must obey his commands (moral and cultic); they are to be moral because he is their Lord, and his will is a moral will.

The people are to be moral because God is experienced as the *determiner of individual and corporate destiny.* Those who follow his ways are rewarded; those who stray from his ways suffer. If the people are not to suffer, they must be moral; if they are to have the benefits of God's promises, they must be moral. God determines the individual and corporate destinies according to the extent to which the people are obedient to the laws that he has commanded.

The prophets experienced God to be *acting in and through historical events* in the community. He uses the might of foreign armies to chastise his people for their waywardness; he uses natural catastrophes to warn them of their transgressions of his moral (and other than moral) laws and will. He calls prophets to interpret the significance of these events in relation to what he is saying and doing through them. Through these interpretations the people are called to repentance and admonished to *follow the true way* of life.

God is spoken of by poets in terms of his *steadfast love and mercy.* The reliability of God's love and mercy was experienced; while God requires moral uprightness and justice, he is also willing to forgive the transgressions of those who are penitent. The corporate and individual lives of his people are never fated to destruction out of God's anger; there is always the *possiblity of turning* from a course of life which is offensive to him into one that is pleasing to him. His steadfast love and mercy is the ground of possibility for rectifying the evils of past and present, and for being freed from the burden of guilt for moral wrongs.

The pastoral imagery of the *shepherd* who cares for his sheep is used to point to the experience of God as a power that wills the well-being of his people. Their lives and deeds are within the overarching concern of their shepherd. Moral life is in the context of not only a framework of laws and rules but also the larger framework of a power and presence that is concerned for the welfare of the people. The people can *live in confidence* that this is so.

In various passages the symbols of *master* and *servant* are used to point to the relation between God and his people. These symbols were fitting expressions of the people's experience of God, for they had duties to perform by virtue of being God's servants. God had authority over them, but this authority was not simply arbitrary; he had made commitments and promises to them that were binding on him. In a proper sense, the relation between God and his people could be spelled out in part in terms of mutual obligations and rights similar to those between a morally responsible master and his servants.

The imagery used to point to the experience of God was not only pastoral and economic. Political symbols were also used. God is the *King* of his people; they are the subjects in his kingdom. As King, God is not only the lawgiver; he is also one who deals justly with his people. Their legislator is also their just judge. His dealings are not only done in accordance with justice; they are also benevolent. He defends the poor and the oppressed; indeed he is experienced as one who has a special concern for the needy. The people are not only to *obey* the laws requiring justice and benevolence; they are also to act justly and benevolently in relations with others because God their King acts justly and benevolently. They are to be *imitators* of God; they are to perceive his work and "go and do likewise."

God was experienced as One who is *Eternal.* Not only were nature and history dependent on him, but also in the face of this experience all that is human, natural, and historical is transitory, as grass that withers in the heat of the sun. For all the symbols and metaphors that seemed appropriate to articulate the human experience of God, he remains a mysterious presence, qualitatively different from man and nature and history. His ways are not human ways, his thoughts are not human thoughts. Thus the human response to him is one of awesome acknowledgment of his majesty and glory; in light of this the human world of experience is temporal, finite, transitory. Humans were called worm's in the light of God's majesty. Nothing in human experience, as valuable and significant as it is, could be given the dignity and value, the sacredness that inheres in God. An attitude of *humility* is called for on the part of all who acknowledge God's power.

The symbols of *teacher* and father were used to articulate the experience of the reality of God. The legislator and commander was also the teacher; his laws and commands were *instruction* in the way in which the people should walk. The frequent use of "the way" as a term to indicate the course of life that was taught is significant. God made known to his people a way of life; he taught them the paths in which they should walk. The language of "the way" suggests both specification with reference to what the people should be and do morally and religiously, and the necessity of continuing to learn from the teacher as new historical "terrain" was confronted in the pilgrimage. God continued to teach through prophets and wise men, through human expounders of the law, through the perceptive interpreters of his "way." The teacher continues to teach, the people continue to be instructed in new circumstances of life.

The familial symbol of God as *father* reflects another dimension of the experience of God's presence. He is a father who shows impartiality in his care and concern for his children, making the rain to fall on the just and the unjust alike, benefiting all without discrimination according to their moral rectitude. He is also a father who cares for the individuality of each of his children, numbering the hairs on their heads. He loves his children, and whom he loves he chastens. Whom he loves he also forgives, receiving them again after their turning from him and providing them the freedom to seek a new moral life. His indignation is real with his children when they do not follow the way, but his wrath never consumes his love. The moral activity of his children is in the context of a relationship similar to that of a loving father and his family.

As I have noted, God is experienced as *love,* as one whose purposes are loving. The Johannine experience of this is particu-

larly central; love becomes the primary but not exclusive characterization of God. His love evokes love, his love is the condition of
the possibility of loving, his love "entails" the obligation to be
loving to others. Moral life is a response to and a modeling of life
and action after his love.

God is the ground of *hope.* "Our hope is in God," the Christian
people could affirm. God provides the newness of possiblities
within human experience; life is not fated to be desperate. There
is the expectation of redemption, of newness, in the midst of guilt
and fear, and death, in the midst of historical catastrophes and
injustices. The future is not foreclosed by the course of events in
the past but offers opportunities to shape new directions, to
discern how individual and corporate life can be fulfilled under
new circumstances. The moral life of the people is lived out in the
context of the experience of hope, the anticipation of the
possibilities for the fulfillment of life in the present and the
future.

From the selective notation of the various symbols used by the
biblical peoples to articulate various dimensions of their experience of the reality of God, it is clear that their lived relationship
with him was the basis of reasons of mind and heart for being
morally serious. My colleague in New York would not articulate
his reasons for being moral in this sort of religious language. He
did not identify himself as one who was in continuity with the
Jewish and Christian communities, and thus their histories had
no authority for him. To him, these notations might have been of
some historical interest, but at best they would have been
religious explanations, and not persuasive justifications for being
moral. The experiences articulated in scripture were not confirmed in and by his own experience. For such accounts to
provide some persuasive reasons (of heart as well as mind) for
being moral, they must be confirmed in the experience of present
generations of people. If they are, then religious reasons exist for
being moral today. To reiterate, the reasons are grounded in the
experience of the reality of God; apart from such experience they
remain matters of historical interest at best.

From this partial account of aspects of the experience of the
biblical people, and on the basis of subsequent and current

experiences of some religious people, a more systematic ordering and development of the theme of this chapter is possible.[3] The primary focus of attention is on religious or, more specifically, Christian life. Basic is the affirmation that the experience of the reality of God evokes, sustains, and renews certain "sensibilities" or "senses," certain sorts of awareness, certain qualities of the human spirit. These in turn .evoke, sustain, and renew moral seriousness and thus provide reasons of the mind and heart for moral life, indeed for a moral life of a qualitatively distinctive sort. Some of the "senses" were introduced in the previous chapter. Since my basic purpose here is different, I shall articulate others, and set them all in a different context. The "senses" I shall elaborate are: a sense of radical dependence, a sense of gratitude, a sense of repentance, a sense of obligation, a sense of possibility, and a sense of direction. These terms are not exhaustive of the Christian life, nor are they precisely coordinated with the "gifts of the Spirit" in the Pauline epistles and the theological virtues developed in Catholic thought.

An ordering of these senses, and of their relations to aspects of the experience of God on the one hand and to moral life on the other, tends to suggest rather external and mechanical relationships, whereas they are related more internally and organically. It tends to suggest a temporal sequence from experience of God to these senses to moral life which is also a distortion of experience. Yet such ordering is necessary for the purposes of clearer exposition. An outline of what follows will aid the reader to keep in mind the pattern and direction of this portion of the chapter.

Each "sense" is correlated with certain dimensions of experiences of God and articulated beliefs about God. Each is also correlated with predispositions to view life and to live in certain ways, and even to act in certain ways morally. The correlations with the theological reference point are as follows. The sense of radical dependence is correlated with the experience of and belief in God as Creator. The sense of gratitude is correlated with the experience of God as beneficent, as good in his creation, sustenance, and redemption of the world. The sense of repentance is correlated with the experience of God as moral authority and as judge. The sense of obligation is correlated with the experience of God as the orderer and sustainer of life. The sense of possibility is correlated with the experience of God as one who continues to act creatively and redemptively, as a God of hope. The sense of direction is correlated with the experience of God as the *telos*, the end of all creation.

This scheme is humanly and theologically too simple. On the theological side it is *one* God who is experienced, whose being, presence, activity, and relatedness to man is not separable into discrete aspects of creator, judge, end, and so forth. Nor can one separate moments of his being judge at one time and end at another. The texture of experience, the theological articulation of it, and even the morality of the religious community become distorted when useful distinctions become separate aspects or moments, such as those that are made between God the Creator and God the Redeemer, or between moments of his creative activity and moments of his redemptive activity. The schema distorts the human reference as well. While, for example, there are moments when the sense of repentance is more overwhelming than the sense of possibility, the two are intricately and intrinsically related in the experience of God.

The correlations of each sense with the more morally significant references are as follows. The sense of dependence is correlated with an awareness of finiteness and with an attitude of trust. Finiteness engenders self-criticism, knowledge of limitations, and recognition of relativity, and limits claims to moral certitude. Trust engenders confidence within the conditions of finiteness; it engenders a sense of responsibility as deputies of the Creator. The sense of gratitude engenders both a reason for being moral and an empowering of the will to do with and for others those actions which are in accord with God's goodness toward humanity. The sense of repentance evokes self-criticism and also a turning toward the moral purposes that are in accordance with perceptions of God's will. The sense of obligation grounds awareness of duties and obligations in moral life and an awareness of personal and social accountability before the ordering power of creation. The sense of possibility counters despair and fatedness and nourishes awareness of opportunities to avoid harm and benefit others. The sense of direction opens paths through the thickets of human experience toward an end that is both spiritual and moral.

There are difficulties in articulating these senses and their relations to moral life, as the perceptive reader has no doubt already observed. The senses are related to viewing life in a moral way, and to acting morally. But precision and clarity in terminology, and in describing the relationships, is extraordinarily difficult. In the reference to morality I am attempting to point to tendencies; whether these are located in the "will" or the "intellect" is not easy to decide. These tendencies have significant consequences for establishing morally serious life, and for the ways in which moral life is lived. But these consequences are not absolutely predictable. "How one lives morally" is related to these senses and to their accompanying tendencies in a moral direction, not only in terms of what persons and communities do, but also in terms of their perspectives on life, their perceptions of what is morally significant about events, their deliberations and their motivations. I can hope only that sufficient indication has been given to what is further developed to provide insight into my intentions.

A Sense of Dependence

In the Christian life, all that is is experienced as being radically dependent upon the author, power, and purpose of life, that is, upon God. Nothing that exists has itself chosen to be: the natural world, individual persons, capacities to develop cultures and societies. To be sure, human agency is involved in the development of what now exists, but in the religious consciousness its being is established by an ultimate power. To be sure, science provides increasingly precise explanations of how individual human persons come into being, develop, and are deceased, and of how the universe of which we are a part developed. The significance of the sense of dependence is not that it provides a causal explanation of how we and the universe we inhabit come into existence. Rather it expresses the experience of necessarily being reliant upon others and upon the Other for life and all of its possibilities. We live in reliance upon parents and children, upon families and friends, upon the continuities and order of nature, upon the social structures and processes that provide the requisites for common life, upon the cultures that humans have developed. In the Christian experience, these are human experiences that open awareness to the Holy, to our ultimate radical dependence upon a power and purpose on whom all things depend.

A sense of dependence is ambiguous with reference to the moral activity of persons. A relationship of dependence upon a superior power or person can become oppressive if it is qualified by the domination of the more dependent party. Out of fear, timidity, or the weakening of confidence to take initiative, freedom and the capacity to innovate can be stifled. A sense of dependence can be the occasion for patronizing attitudes on the part of the superior power; it can subtly destroy human vitality and self-respect in forms of paternalism. The sense of radical dependence can foster personal and moral immaturity.

The absence of a sense of dependence also has its perilous consequences. Without awareness of the reliance that persons or communities have on other persons, institutions, and the ordering of the world of nature, there is a temptation to a false autonomy, to a self-sufficiency that can lead to destructive consequences for others and for the world. Consciousness of this, I believe, is evident in the recovery of the sense of dependence the human race has upon the other biological species and on the limited natural resources of the earth. Without a sense of dependence persons and communities are prone to exploit others, to claim a right to determine for others what is best for them, to be falsely secure in their judgments and to be excessively certain about the rightness of their actions.

The experience of radical dependence on God in the Jewish and Christian traditions has been expressed in different theological terms. There have been expositions of divine determination not only of the trends of life but also of all specific events in life which turn dependence into passivity. In contrast there have been those for whom dependence upon God is "historically" and "existentially" remote; a power was needed to create, but once creation exists a radical autonomy exists for man. It would be interesting to analyze how different interpretations of creation's dependence upon the Creator can be correlated with different nuances in the human experience of dependence (immediately on God, mediately on God, remotely on God), and in turn with different reasons for being moral and different moral outlooks, but such a study would take us afield. A brief proposal that involves normative theological judgments is more in order.

The heart of the matter in Christian and also, I believe, in Jewish experience is the affirmation that the power on which all depends is good (including morally good), and wills the well-being of his creation. Thus the sense of dependence is formed (intellectually and affectively) by the relationship to God who is construed in these terms. If God is powerful, but is man's enemy and destroyer, if he is a power of evil, the sense of dependence would be qualitatively different; we would be trapped by a necessary reliance on one whom we fear. The Christian belief about God's goodness, if confirmed in individual experience, qualifies the human sense of dependence.

The belief that God is good and wills the well-being of his creation does not in this cryptic form resolve all the experiential and intellectual issues. Two vast and ancient questions remain: (1) To what extent does God's power determine the particular occasions and the general order of the world? Obversely, to what extent must account be taken of the human capacities to determine particular occasions and the general order? And (2) What constitutes the well-being of the creation, including humanity? How is this well-being known? Unsophisticated responses to these questions must suffice here. To the first I respond with an accent upon man's capacities to act, to exercise initiative in ordering events within a reliance upon and interaction with God's power, presence, and activity. To the second I respond with the affirmation that the well-being of creation is constituted by many values, many qualities, and that the exploration and realization of this well-being is a continuous task in which our species has a particular obligation by virtue of what it has developed to be. What constitutes the well-being is never completely known; what insight into it we have comes through the dynamics of human experience, past and present.

The reason for being moral that can be articulated from this sense of dependence is not one that is currently popular, nor is it without the possibilities of debasing human life. (Within the multiform character of the experience of God, it is also modified by other aspects.) It is that the people owe allegiance to the one who provides them with life and its possibilities. To be the recipient of life is to have a sense of indebtedness to the giver of life. It is to be oriented toward nature and other persons in an attitude of custodianship, of deputyship, for all that is and is to be is given and not earned, available and not possessed. The human community is the caretaker and the cultivator of what has been given out of God's goodness. Since the giver is good, however, and wills the well-being of what he has made possible, and since mankind has developed the capacities to act intentionally, to cultivate the earth, the religious sense of dependence is not a cowering subservience to God. The sense of dependence grounds two aspects of the moral outlooks and attitudes of Christians: their awareness of human limitation, and their ultimacy of confidence.

Man, in the context of Western religions, is never fully autonomous. This is reflected in the moral outlooks and attitudes of members of the Christian community. (Indeed, the theological error in some of the theologies of radical secularity that enjoyed brief popularity a decade ago was precisely the failure to recognize the limits of human autonomy, the implications of man's dependence upon God.) Human life and action are in the context of relations of interdependency not only with other persons, but with social organization, culture, and nature. To rely upon others, and ultimately to rely upon God, is to experience the limits of self-sufficiency, and thus to recognize the finitude of one's self, others, and all that is. The awareness of finitude, in the context of a sense of dependence on others and on God, has rational and deeply personal implications for moral life.

As theologians, and particularly Protestant theologians, have long noted, the absolutizing of objects of loyalty short of God—including particular moral values and principles—is the temptation of finite man. It is the traditional sin of idolatry, the error that makes the security of persons and communities rest upon their certitude that they are the sole custodians of what is true and right and good. The experiential awareness of finiteness requires that we recognize that what we know about moral values, and what we state as perduring moral principles, is relative to our created human experience. Thus while it is possible to have a considerable certitude that certain moral values are "almost absolute," that certain moral principles are to be adhered to with only a few exceptions, nonetheless persons and communities cannot claim intrinsic freedom from error. They cannot assume an attitude of dogmatism about their firmest moral convictions. Moral life is a finite human enterprise; the formulation of moral values and principles is not exempt from that condition.

The sense of dependence, and the awareness of finitude require and nourish an outlook of persistent self-criticism in the moral life. There must be an openness to re-evaluation of moral beliefs, of principles, and particularly of choices that have been made. Frequent use of the subjunctive mode is fitting in addressing events and issues. The temptation to fix historically relative perceptions and teachings into eternally valid rules of conduct must be resisted. Willingness freely to admit moral mistakes is in order.

There is a more active or positive aspect to the awareness of finitude as well. It establishes a readiness to explore freshly the possibilities that are present in new circumstances of life to avoid ancient and new evils, and to achieve new patterns of well-being. A willingness to learn, a readiness to resist premature foreclosure of reflection, is required. Without lusting for novelty for its own sake, persons and communities can entertain the possibilities of new or different moral requirements under new and changing conditions of relationships to society, to the natural world, and to other persons. In short, awareness of human limitation restrains the human tendency to impose uncritically upon tomorrow the moral certitudes that were sufficient for another time, another cultural place, another historical circumstance. At the same time it evokes a readiness to search out the moral requirements that are related to present and impending circumstances, that are required by current developments in society and culture, that light the way through the dark moral forest in which we live.

In a way that perhaps baffles those for whom the experience of the reality of God is foreign, the dependence of man upon God engenders trust and confidence as well as self-criticism. The pastoral imagery of the ancient Semitic people makes this point more vividly than does more abstract language. To be dependent upon God is to be like sheep who can rely upon the shepherd. It is to live in the confidence that there is one who accepts ultimate accountability for human life and all of creation, one who wills that their care and sustenance be provided, one who seeks their well-being. This confidence is a ground for an inner freedom that religious persons often experience—a freedom to accept their finitude and the anxieties that accompany it, a freedom to be and to act under conditions of less than complete control and certainty, a freedom to preserve what is of value and to risk what might be lost in the thrust of life into a dimly known future. The courage, the freedom, the willingness to seek the right and the good under finite conditions is sustained by this confidence.

This confidence provides a reason of heart and mind to be morally serious in a particular sense and way. The point can be made as follows. If there is an ultimate power on whom humans can depend, and if the propriety of the sense of dependence is confirmed in the experience of persons, then those persons who have confidence in the reliability of God ought to be reliable in their relations to others who depend upon them for some of their well-being. Experientially, there is a readiness to be reliable, trustworthy persons in relation to others. Imperatively, in the light of the dependability of God in whom persons have confidence, they ought to be dependable in relations to others who rely upon them. This "ought" pertains not only to the attitude of reliability but also to the particular duties and obligations that are incumbent upon persons in the network of dependence that is the condition of human life.

A Sense of Gratitude

To write about the sense of dependence that an experience of the reality of God evokes without introducing the sense of gratitude has not been easy, for the power of life on which we depend is one whose will for his creation is its well-being. That the ultimate power is good is the key affirmation on which the response of thankfulness turns. This affirmation is only in part confirmed in human experience; the occasions in natural, social, and individual life which count against an unconditioned certitude of God's goodness are too many and too personally poignant to be blithely dismissed. The human quarrel with God that led the suffering Job and Jeremiah to curse the days that they were born is, in all honesty, a continuing quarrel. To be grateful to God for life is difficult when cherished human life is painfully and brutally taken away, when the needs of the bodies of countless persons are not adequately met, when whole communities of persons are subjected to programs of extinction, when injustices reign under the domination of the powerful and the rich. That God is good, and therefore deserves human gratitude, is a reasonable affirmation of faith and hope, only partially confirmed in experience. Only cheap religious rhetoric could deny that trust in God's goodness requires a step from what is verified in experience to a riskier and deeper faith, a step from the promises of goodness that we feel have been kept to a hope for the future fulfillment of God's will of well-being of creation.

As with the sense of dependence, so in the sense of gratitude the goodness provided by the natural world, by cultures and societies, by other persons, is the glass through which religious persons perceive the goodness of God. The occasions of thankfulness to others for what they have done for us are at the same time the occasions for thankfulness to God, as all the great prayers of thanksgiving in the life of the church make clear. Though these occasions seem to come in small sizes and with less frequency than we desire, nonetheless they testify to the religious consciousness of the goodness of life, and even provoke communities to celebration. For all of the anxieties and struggles of living, we are grateful to be, to exist. In certain moments of experience we recognize that we have been loved by others beyond our deserving, we have been forgiven when we dared not believe it was possible, we have been sustained by the patience of others when they have had sufficient reasons to reject us, we have benefited from nature and society more than we have contributed to them. We have received more than we have earned or deserved, and we are thankful. In the religious consciousness these are experiences that open the possibility of affirming the goodness of God; they confirm his goodness which we only dimly and in part apprehend.

Gratitude as a reason of mind and heart for being moral has been a deep and persistent one in the biblical communities and in the life and thought of the church. "Freely you have received, freely give" is more than a convenient saying to induce church-goers to place money in an offering basket during worship. The comma, in a sense, covers the fulcrum of a way of life. In its affective dimensions, the sense of gratitude moves the will to act. Having freely received, the community and its members are moved to give freely. It also has imperative dimensions which ground a command in the isness of experience: you have freely received, therefore you ought to give freely. Only the myopia of an individualistic pietism would confine the significance of this to individual acts of mercy. Out of gratitude for the beneficence of God to a nation, to a people, a beneficence that is beyond their rights to claim a just reward for virtue, nations and peoples ought to share what they have. To see implications of a sense of gratitude for more than corporate and individual benevolence is not too strained; out of a sense of gratitude should come a concern for justice. Having received, a people should not take more than is their due; they should not deprive others of life's resources for the sake of their own luxurious pleasures and conveniences. It is out of a sense of gratitude that both moral volition and an imperative arise. God has freely given life to us; we, in thankfulness to him, are to be concerned for others' well-being as he has been concerned for ours.

The sense of gratitude, like the sense of dependence, can be oppressive and destructive if it leads to an obsequious and nig-gardly cowering before those who have given to us. The intentions of the human giver can be to create an oppressive dependence in the receivers out of which absolute loyalties are claimed and tyrannical dominance is exercised. Thus, the sense of gratitude is ambiguous for moral life. But gratitude can also be liberating. If the gifts we receive are graciously and freely given, given in love rather than as covers for the demonic intentions of self-glorification of the giver and for his dominance, we experience joyful and grateful freedom in relation to the giver, and in relation to what is given. The importance of the Christian belief in God as gracious needs to be noted here; God is experienced and articulated in terms of grace—of a free giving of life and newness of life. The ultimate power over against us is a gracious and benevolent power. What is given to humankind is given in his love; it is not merely what we deserve by our accomplishments but is there for our response, our participation, our tending and use.

On the pivot of the experience of gratitude to God and to other persons turns the moral life of members of the Christian community. Not only is the will moved; not only is there an imperative to give to and care for others. Also certain sorts of caring for the world are implied. If we have received life and its benefits from God's goodness, in a living gratitude what is available to us is not ours to serve only our own interests, to mutilate, to exhaust, to destroy wantonly, to deprive others of. Rather receiving life and the natural and cultural worlds of which we are a part in gratitude to its gracious and loving giver turns us to care for it, to care for others near and distant, to be concerned for the well-being of future as well as present generations. Life and its benefits are to be shared freely, justly, and lovingly.

I believe that this is at the heart of religious morality in the Western world. When religious morality has taken the forms of precise determinations in laws and rules, this has been done to spell out what a thankful community ought to do. When it has been taught in terms of spontaneous deeds of loving service, this too has been understood to stem from gratitude. God has been good to human persons and communities; in thankfulness to him we have reason enough to seek the well-being of others, to honor their rights, to fulfill our natural duties and our obligations to them. In thankfulness we are moved to do so. This theme is central in the morality and ethics of both Judaism and Christianity. As we shall see in the conclusion of this chapter, it is one aspect of the ethics of the imitation of God. God has done good things for us; in thankfulness we are to "go and do likewise."

A Sense of Repentance

The recorded history of man's experience of God in the great Western religions is replete with indications of man's need for, and experience of, repentance. In penitential psalms, in the writings of theologians both great and modest in their historical significance, in the cultic practices, in responses of religious communities to social injustices and catastrophes, and in other ways, the persistence of a sense of repentance can be demonstrated. Persons and communities have ignored and denied their dependence upon God and his goodness. They have been curved in on themselves and used persons, the natural world, and institutions excessively for their own interests and desires. They have crippled and destroyed the physical and spiritual lives of others by their greed, their lust for domination, their excessive certitude about the righteousness of their causes. They have exerted dominion over the earth, as they have been called to do, but have ignored the relations of dependance that are part of this vocation. They have been spoilers rather than tenders of the natural world, they have been dictators rather than deputies and servants in relation to others, they have been dominators rather than participants with others in the ordering of life. In short, they have put other gods before their beneficent Creator.

God is experienced as the Judge. Men and communities are guilty before him. He calls them to repentance. Life has been wantonly taken that he wills to be sustained and fulfilled. The way of life that men have been taught in their experience and perceptions of God's purposes has been violated. Both the social injustices built into the patterns of human affairs which violate the rights of persons and groups and the individual acts of injustice are dissonant with the justice of God. In the biblical accounts the law and the prophets both call men to repentance; this call was central to the teachings of Jesus and to the writings of the Christian scripture. It has been a persistent call since the closing of the canon. The call strikes a responsive note in those who experience the reality of God; we are aware of the tension, if not the outright contradiction, between what God has done in his goodness and what we have done as agents in nature and history. We experience the ultimate power as our Judge standing over against us. Before God man stands in guilt. We have a "sense" of repentance.

As with other aspects of man's experience of the reality of God, so with the sense of repentance the occasions of human experience are the mediators of the deeper and more universal dimensions. Parents often recognize when they have been unfair to their children, when they have treated them as possessions rather than as gifts to be nourished, when they have wounded their spirits. Husbands and wives often sense when they have violated the integrity of their partners, when they have been unfaithful in meeting their commitments to love, honor, and cherish each other. Friends often are acutely conscious of the little deceptions and dishonesties that are not in accord with the unwritten obligations that exist in the relationship of friendship. The white community in America and elsewhere occasionally comes to an acute recognition of the institutional and legal as well as personal ways in which it has suppressed the rights and frustrated the aspirations of Indians, Blacks, Chicanos, and others. Nations sense a need to acknowledge their wrongs to other nations and to persons. For all its philosophical difficulties, the notion of corporate guilt for the genocidal policies of Nazi Germany resonated with many postwar German people. Similarly, many American people feel that as a nation we bear accountability for the unjust destruction of persons, of a social fabric, and of nature during the war in Southeast Asia. Many participants in the technological culture of the modern world, with all its comforts and benfits, are increasingly conscious of their exploitations and pollutions of the natural world, and of the dismal legacy they are bequeathing to subsequent generations.

The religious consciousness, with its perceptions of the reality of a power present and active through these relationships and events, acknowledges a violation of man's relation to God in the violations of proper relations between persons, between nations and social groups, and between human culture and the natural world. Sins against others and against nature are sins against

God; they express a disordering of relations which is basically a disorder in man's relations to God. Accountability is not only between persons but between man and God. The sense of repentance is ultimately the acknowledgment of guilt before God. We are judged not merely by others, and by the consequences of our actions upon others; through these we are judged by God.

Repentance is not self-recrimination; it is not wallowing in masochistic guilt feelings, enjoying the humiliation of our failures. It is more than the acknowledgment of guilt; it is a turning. The call to repentance is not only the invocation of a judgment; it is also, in biblical language, a call "to return unto the Lord." It is a turning again to the purposes of personal and common life that are consonant with God's good purposes and deeds. It is to engage in those actions that sustain, enhance, and fulfill the well-being of the creation and particularly the human community. Like the senses of dependence and gratitude, it grounds a reason of mind and heart for moral seriousness and moral action. We ought to be reoriented toward those ends from which we have turned; we ought to govern our relations in accordance with those values and principles we have violated. We ought to turn toward these because of a recognition that straying from them causes undue harm to others that is not in accord with God's will and way. There is also a more personal and emotive aspect of the sense of repentance that is important for moral life. The ultimate power is one that "blots out our transgressions," that does not ultimately count our sins against us, that renews our desires and capacities to seek and do what is morally right and good as well as forgives us our trespasses. The sense of repentance moves our capacities to action.

Our senses of dependence and gratitude are nourished by repentance: dependence upon the opportunities and capacities provided us to alter our courses of life, gratitude for opportunities to restore disrupted relations through forgiveness, for occasions to rectify the corporate and individual misdeeds of the past. Other "senses" could be distinguished and elaborated: a sense of humility is fostered in recognition of the harmful deeds we have done, and in the recognition that we will do more such deeds in the future. Humility in the religious life is not a crippling fear to act in the light of the mistakes one might possibly make. Rather it is a readiness to revise one's purposes, to acknowledge one's mistakes, to redress the harmful consequences of one's past actions. It takes the form of willingness to question one's own judgments, to listen to others whose wisdom and insight might help us. It is not accident that the prophet Micah joins humility with justice and kindness in the well-known words, "He has showed you, O man, what is good; and what does the Lord require of you but to do justice, and to love kindness, and to walk humbly with your God?" (Micah 6:8).

A sense of freedom is also grounded in repentance. Martin Luther's forceful celebration of the freedom of the "inner man" is confirmed in the experience of many Christians. The assurance of God's mercy and love for man that are not overcome even by man's turning from God is realized in the forgiveness that is part of repentance. This freedom is not the freedom to pursue one's whims, though such aberrations of life are recorded from the earliest Christian congregations to the present. Rather it is a freedom to act willingly in accordance with God's purposes, to risk oneself in being for others; to exercise one's capacities even when final certitude of the rightness of one's principles and values is elusive. The attitudes and even the actions of religious persons may be qualified by these "senses."

A Sense of Obligation

The experience of the reality of God evokes a sense of moral obligation in persons and in the religious community. This is grounded in part in human dependence upon and gratitude to God and has been assumed as a condition necessary for a sense of repentance. It deserves special attention, however, in part to indicate some of the significance for morality of the experience of God as an ordering and sustaining power.

The language of duties and obligations, and the attitude of being obligated to do certain things, are clearly somewhat suspect in parts of contemporary culture. To those who equate moral maturity with spontaneous abundance of morally approvable desires, the sense of obligation appears to be a deficiency of character. To persons who believe that they ought to do only what they immediately desire to do, living with a strong sense of duties and obligations seems repressive, alienating, and inauthentic. Evidences and reasons that support the critical response to an ethics of duties and obligations are worthy of consideration. The moral life has too frequently been depicted as one of bending one's inclinations to purely rational principles of morality in such a way as to create severe and debilitating tensions within persons. It has too frequently been taught as a bending of one's will, one's desires, one's sense of integrity to the extrinsic authority of others who by virtue of their social roles and status claim the right to assert unequivocally what is right and who demand obedience only under threat of punishment. Consciences have been deformed, initiative on the part of persons has been stifled, spontaneity has been repressed, capacities to act have been crippled. Morality has been taught as primarily negative rather than positive in its ultimate aims. The Adolf Eichmanns of this world have used their senses of obligation to authority to justify horrendously evil deeds. While these and other evidences of debilitating consequences of a morality that is exclusively carried by a sense of obligation and duty require careful consideration, there are also reasons and evidences for sustaining such a sense.

Human experience in interrelations with others, both in more personal communities and in complex institutional settings, leads to awareness of duties and obligations that must be met for the sake of individual and common good. There are natural duties that we have by virtue of our roles in society: parents have duties to their children to nourish and sustain their physical and spiritual lives to the best of their ability. Professors have obligations to their students and to their administrators as a result of their contracting to fulfill this professional role, just as physicians have obligations to patients, lawyers to clients, and so forth. Failure to fulfill these duties and obligations usually creates personal and social harm. In social and political life there is an obligation to seek justice, to render to persons and groups what they are due, to develop legal and economic policies that tend to treat equals equally. Failure to have a sense of obligation to seek justice deprives whole communities of the liberties others claim for themselves, deprives large segments of the population of the benefits of the natural and cultural worlds. The frustration of justice leads to social unrest, quite properly, on the part of those unjustly deprived. A sense of obligation to even the laws of the natural world is coming to our consciousness. Since our well-being, and that of future generations, depends upon conforming our activities to a greater extent than in the past to the requisite balance of various natural forces, we feel obligated to constrain our exploitative tendencies.

The experience of the ultimate power as the sustainer and orderer of life is mediated through our experience of the require-ments of life to be sustained and ordered, and to be sustaining and ordering in relation to others. While we cannot argue that evidence of the need for sustaining and ordering activities and structures is sufficient evidence for the existence of God, we can affirm that the religious consciousness discerns the presence of God in such ordering. It infers from this that humankind is obligated to him to attend to the proper ordering of life. Various traditions in Christian morality have developed this basic point in ways that are subject to critical scrutiny from both theological and ethical perspectives. There has been some tendency to think about a moral *order* that God has established; an order of creation tends to be interpreted as static and immutable, and thus the dynamism and development of life is insufficiently appreci-ated. The articulation of the order*ing* activity and presence of God guards against such notions, and is truer to the perception of God as active power and presence rather than as eternal, that is, nontemporal, and immutable being. There is a constant tempta-tion to claim an infallible perception of what the moral order is, and thus to prescribe with moral certitude what actions and patterns of relations are in conformity with it. Our affirmation that even in its religious dimensions moral activity and under-standing is part of human and finite experience precludes such certitude on grounds that could be developed epistemologically. A further temptation is to identify the order that exists in human relations at a particular time and place with the order that God created, for example, male domination over women, or monar-chical forms of government. The principal errors in this from a theological perspective are the failures to account for the "distance" between God and the social world, to recognize the human creative and corrupting aspects of the social world, and the developmental character of experience and understanding of what God's ordering requires.

One can articulate the experience of God as sustainer and orderer in more dynamic and temporal-historical terms. God is sustaining and ordering. God's purposes are not revealed in full clarity in a single moment of history or experience, but through human participation in nature and society together with a conscientious wrestling to perceive and discern them. We are obligated to God, we have a duty to God to seek to discern his sustaining and ordering will, and to shape the purposes of our actions in their light. We discern through experience the divine will for justice. God's purposes are just. We have a sense of obligation to God and to others to seek to develop an ordering of life that is more just than what exists. God's justice is not arbitrary; justice is a requirement of the moral and nonmoral goodness and fulfillment of life that God wills for his creation. We are *obligated* to seek justice even when it is detrimental to our immediate interests and desires, and to those of our people and our generation. To experience God as orderer and sustainer is to have a sense of obligation, to have a reason of mind and heart, for being moral. Our obligation is both to him and to the creation he orders and sustains.

The richer theological context of the sense of obligation must be noted. Our relation to God is not only one of obligation. We are obligated to the power that creates benefits, to the God to whom we are grateful. We are obligated to him through our obligations to others who also sustain us, and to whom we are grateful. Our obligations are in the wider and richer context of the experience of God who is loving, and who is gracious. They are in the context of a relation of trust and of love. To lose sight of this is to court the error of a religious morality built only on a sense of duty to God, only on a threat of divine judgment and punishment. Our sense of obligation is to a gracious power who wills the well-being of his creation; it is to others who are the agents of that will in relation to us and to the world of which we are a part.

A Sense of Possibilities

The experience of the reality of God as articulated in Judaism and Christianity includes the perception that the ultimate power standing over against us continues to create the conditions in which new possibilities of life and experience can occur, and in which the redemption, the renewal, and the partial fulfillment of the old can take place. God is not only the orderer and limiter; he is also the continuing power of creativity, and in response to that power the human religious consciousness has a sense of possibilities. A practical maxim might be stated: the Christian community and its members are obliged to seek in their particular historic and natural circumstances what God is requiring and enabling them to do. The enabling has a double reference: it refers to the empowering of capacities to act but also to the development of the occasions in which new and different actions are possible. The "sense of possibilities" refers both to the agent, the person who responds to others and events, and to the "other," the persons, relations, events, and states of affairs to which persons respond.

Religious morality that views the task of mankind to be one of exclusively conserving the values that have been achieved, or acting to conform events to relatively static and closed precepts derived from past experience, distorts the richness of the experience of God. In the distinction of Bergson, used also by Tielhard de Chardin and others, such morality becomes closed rather than open. The sense of possibility, correlated as it is with the experience of some significant ongoing creativity on the part of the ultimate power, in contrast recognizes that historically institutions and cultures change or develop, that persons alter in the course of the many relationships and significant events in their lives, and that the natural, biological heritage of humanity is an ongoing process.

Religious morality that views the task of mankind to require a unique perception of what ought to be done under the ever changing circumstances of life accents openness and draws heavily on the sense of possibility. Unqualified openness is fraught with as many errors as is closed morality. It assumes that the continuities of the experiences of persons are not significant sources of moral insight, that men have histories (in the special sense of acting in strictly unrepeatable ways) but no natures, that there are no significant analogies to be drawn between the events and actions of one time and place to that of another. It has, theologically, a view of God as utterly free, or as bound only to the revelation in Christ that he has chosen to be bound to; in light of this the possibilities of his command or activities being radically different under different conditions is stressed. In short, taken by itself the experience of the continuing creative and renewing presence and activity of God is only a partial one; the power that creates possibilities is also the ordering and sustaining power. Correlated with this is a morality: the people have reasons of mind and heart to be open to new occasions which might require different actions, but the new possiblities are not discontinuous with what has gone on before.

The experience that the ultimate power is the ground and condition of some significant openness, of possibilities to act, of the opportunities to search out new ways to direct the course of events, of the probability of different benefits for the human race, is mediated by human experience. If there were no development in persons, nature, and culture there would be reason to articulate the experience of God as a static, impassive, and immutable being. If persons were perceived to be dramatically and utterly determined or fated to be what they are, if it were not possible to affirm that "had I chosen to do such and so, I would be different from what I am," then the ultimate power would be experienced as a fate. The experience that choices of persons to exercise political, economic, and military power have directed the course of historical events, that intentional interventions in the processes of nature have had significant consequences for individuals (for example, medication and surgery) and for larger arenas of the natural world (for example, the denuding of forest lands by men), establishes the condition which makes it plausible to believe that God grounds the possibilities for action. In these possibilities are the opportunities to be open to personal change, to direct events toward more just and benevolent ends, to intervene in nature so as to avoid some harms and to create some benefits. Thus in response to God religious men and communities have a sense of possibilities. They are agents who have the capacity and the obligation to exercise powers available to them in the ways that are being made possible, and in accord with what the community and individuals discern God's purposes to be.

A Sense of Direction

Pre-Reformation Christianity and the continuing Catholic tradition articulated the experience of God (with the aid of symbols drawn from classic Greek philosophy) as an orientation toward the ultimate end, the *telos* of both persons and the rest of creation. A basic understanding of human life is imbedded in this, namely, that persons are inherently directed toward their true end, and that particular actions are actions toward particular ends. The experience, however, is not a Roman Catholic possession; it is more universal in the consciousness of Christians. The experience of God sustains a sense of direction in human life. God is the end, the *telos*; he is the "object" toward which life is drawn and toward which it can be directed through human acts.

Integrity and coherence in individual lives is in large measure dependent upon the consistency of intentions that persons have, not only in terms of specifically intended and articulated purposes, but also in terms of the orientation of the "will" toward certain ends. Personal life looks forward, corporate life looks forward; what persons and communities do and become is determined in a significant measure by the ends toward which they look and move. This orientation does not preclude interest in and concern for the antecedents of activity, but it stresses a direction toward the future, toward purposive ends to be realized. We create visions, and are drawn in our activity by our aspirations for the future of man and society and nature; we are creatures of *eros*, of a love that draws us toward the objects of our deepest desires. The actions of persons and communities over a period of time express to observers what the visions, the aspirations, the ends of their lives are; they make clear the objects of the most profound loves.

The experience of religious persons includes an awareness that the ultimate power of creation is its ultimate end, that man (to take recourse to an ancient theme of *exitus et reditus*) and all creation come from and return to God. This religious experience, and the view of life articulated from it, is not only expressed in the mystical tendencies and aspirations of Christians; it is also expressed in a moral way of life. God is our end; directed toward him as our end there is a longing, a desire, an aspiration to act and to order life in accordance with God's purposes for man. To allude to the religious vision of Jonathan Edwards, there is a love of beings which is open to the love of Being itself; there is a love of Being which orients us to other beings—persons, communities, events—so that we seek their good. A receptive and passive openness to the reality of God, perhaps a mystical aspect of experience, orients men toward him so that their moral actions and purposes are also oriented by this vision of God and love for God. Charles Wesley could sing of a "love divine, all loves excelling" which men have received, and this evokes a love for God, an orientation toward him; it also nourishes a love for what he has created and an orientation toward its well-being. For the religious consciousness God is the ultimate object of human desires and loves; he is the end toward which life is oriented, and in this orientation human desires and loves have a sense of direction. The love men receive is mediated by the goodness of the created world, by the love of others; the love of God is expressed through man's proper love of the created world, and of other persons.

The Catholic tradition has long understood that the wrong objects of human intentions and love leads to the wrong actions in moral life. If the chief end of man is to fulfill maximally the natural desires for sensual pleasure, and if persons are used as means to that fulfillment, life will show a consistency, it will have a sense of direction. Actions, however, will not redound to the benefit of the human community but only to the satisfaction of the sensual desires of individuals so oriented. If a nation is oriented toward the end of its increase in power and the rewards that power can bring to its people, its activities of military, economic, and political domination will demonstrate a sense of direction. Its actions, however, will not bring about the fruits of justice, peace, and benevolence. If the ultimate end of the scientific enterprise is to bring all things under human control, to make man the ultimate power, perils will be courted which are potentially disastrous to the well-being of creation. The objects of the deepest human longings, of the most dominant and pervasive human desires, to a great extent determine the worthiness of specific human acts. The ends toward which action is directed are crucial; improper ends misdirect activities with reference to the well-being of persons, culture, societies, and nature.

To be experientially oriented toward God provides a sense of direction in moral life. Man *is* oriented toward God—this becomes an affirmation that is plausible on the basis of reflection about human experience. Man ought to be oriented toward God in his activities—this becomes an imperative. To be so directed is to will that all one's actions—one's intentions, the means of action and how they are exercised, and the consequences of action—glorify God. Praising the ultimate power is only part of the religious life. More significant for our puposes is to recognize that being directed by those moral principles that are in accordance with God's purposes, seeking to realize those moral values that are in accord with what we believe God values, constitutes a life that glorifies God. The experience of God as the end of creation, and the articulations of human perceptions of the God who is the *telos*, provide a sense of direction in moral life. That God is the end becomes the ground of a reason of mind and heart for being moral, and a direction for the activity that is warranted by that reason.

The Imitation of God

Many themes have historically been stated as central to a moral life that is grounded in religious experience and religious reasons. The centrality, if not the exclusivity, of love has been one; others have been living out our justification by faith, conforming life to the moral order of creation, exercising our Christian freedom, living in the context of God's promises, and doing God's humanizing work. Yet others could be cited. The simplification that such systematization creates is not always persuasive on theological grounds, and often has unfortunate consequences ethically. Thus it is with some uncertainty that I would propose a theme that is consistent with the religious reasons of mind and heart for being moral as I have attempted to order them. Surely all I can propose is that the theme of the imitation of God is a central one. It cannot be exclusive in a narrow sense because it incorporates many themes stated by other accounts of theological ethics. Nor would I defend it because it is an inclusive theme. Rather its centrality, I believe, arises from the experience of the biblical communities, and from the religious communities that are heirs to the biblical legacy.

The term imitation can easily be misleading. It appears to permit no initiative on the part of the agent who is imitating God; it appears to suggest a portrait of the paradigmatic way of life that is a master Xerox copy. The believer's relation to God would seem to require that he do the impossible, that is, copy the activity of God. Because of these misleading possibilities, with reference to Jesus Christ, many Protestants prefer to write about Christian discipleship, about *Nachfolge Christi* (following of Christ) rather than *imitatio Christi.*

If what I have written warrants the generalization that the religious reasons for morality lead to the centrality of an ethics of the imitation of God, it ought to be clear that the use of "imitation" in this chapter is not meant to refer to an external aping. The form is more like: "God has done *a, b,* and *c* for the well-being of the human community and the whole creation; those who have experienced the reality of God's *a, b,* and *c* are moved and required to do similar things for others." To fore-shorten what is more complex, it can be said that God is dependable; in dependence on his reliability, religious persons are moved to be and ought to be dependable in their relations to others. God is beneficent; he acts for the well-being of the creation. In gratitude for his beneficence to men and the world, men are moved to and ought to act for the benefits of other persons, society, and the natural world. God judges human failures and offers forgiveness and the possibilities for renewal of life; Christians are moved to and ought to be forgiving, to seek rectification for their moral misdeeds, and to lead a "new" moral life. God is ordering and sustaining his creation; Christians are moved and ought to be agents acting for an ordering of life in accordance with God's work and purposes. The pattern of imitation is thus clear. The fundamental pattern does not determine precisely what the religious community and its members are to do under particular circumstances. It is not for human eyes to see precisely and concretely what God does here or there, since others are always the mediating agents of his activity and purposes. And these agents are human—finite, fallible, and turned in on themselves. The fundamental pattern does not dissolve the need for persons and communities to be purposive agents, responsible for seeking what is required. It does, however, indicate the connection that is at the heart of the religious reasons for being moral. God has done such and such for the well-being of creation; go and do likewise. God seeks justice for the weak and the fatherless; God seeks to maintain the rights of the afflicted and the destitute; God seeks to rescue the weak and the needy; God seeks their deliverance from the hand of the wicked. Go and do likewise. God has met man's deepest needs in love; men thus are to meet the deepest needs of their neighbors in love.

My companion in the Lexington Avenue bar would not have felt complimented if I had told him he had acted in imitation of God, or that God was glorified by his actions. Nor would he have been pleased if I had told him he was an anonymous Christian. My theological sophistication might permit me to say these things about him and about what he did. Also, it is fitting for me to be thankful to God for him and for what he did. But to prove him to be "religious" in some "generic" sense is not the point of this book. Rather, if one does experience the reality of God, and articulates it in Christian concepts and symbols, what he did was the sort of thing that Christians ought to do. The sort of person he was is the sort of person Christians ought to be. The religious consciousness has reasons of mind and heart to be morally serious, and to act for the well-being of others at cost to oneself.

If one is religious in Christian and Jewish traditional senses, there are sufficient and compelling reasons to be moral. These reasons might even color or accent the ways in which one is moral, and acts morally. But one is not religious for reasons of morality. Why be religious? To attempt even to suggest what might be persuasive answers to that question is a task of apologetic theology, and is not undertaken here.

5 Theological Interpretation of the Significance of Circumstances

In the analysis of the incident in New York, I noted that beliefs held by the moral agent function in part to enable him to evaluate what was significant in the interactions that were going on in the bar. Although my companion was not an intellectual, and would not have been concerned to articulate, in concepts, the beliefs that were important to him, it is possible to infer from his actions what some of his significant beliefs were. Obviously he believed in honesty and fairness; the significance of the first interaction he observed between the soldier and the bartender was that the bartender had cheated the young man. The circumstances were evaluatively described as an occasion in which something dishonest and unfair was occurring. The significance of the circumstances was determined by such a conviction on his part. In this part of the sequence of events there would not have been much disagreement by observers; the incorrect change, unless given by mistake, would lead most persons to describe the circumstances in similar ways. Another level of reflection could be articulated: in the evaluation of the circumstances a concept of honesty or fairness was instrumental and decisive in determining what was morally significant.

The judgment that the incorrect change was not a mistake but deliberate and therefore blameworthy was apparently based on some previous experiences of my colleague. Bartenders in New York are likely to do such a thing. A similar prejudgment was made about the cab driver; to insure against certain possible harm being done to the drunken soldier a series of information about the cabbie and his passenger was recorded. From there another inference seems warranted. My colleague appears to have believed at least the following: persons dealing with drunks in New York are quite susceptible to the temptation to take advantage of their condition and to gain for themselves by dishonest deeds. Perhaps a more inclusive inference is warranted. Persons are sufficiently corrupt to lead one to believe that if there is no surveillance of their activities they are likely to take advantage of others for the sake of their own gain. My companion probably had a "visceral" conviction about the corruption of his fellow citizens; certainly he did not have a *concept* of the human moral state that was consciously used to interpret the moral significance of these circumstances. I doubt that he would have used the term or symbol of "sin" to denote his conviction. Yet it is clear, I believe, that a "notion" of human corruption determined in part his interpretation and depiction of what was going on in those circumstances, or of what might occur if precautions were not taken. This evaluative description of the significance of the sequence shaped his own moral response to it. The formal point to be drawn is that beliefs and convictions are more or less clearly symbolized and conceptualized; these symbols and conceptions function to interpret the significance of the circumstances in which action occurs. Certain symbols and concepts highlight the moral significances of the circumstances and in turn determine, at least in part, what the response of the morally conscientious person will be.

The thesis of this chapter follows. Religious symbols and theological concepts are used to interpret the significance of other persons, of events, and of the circumstances in which action is possible and required. Some symbols and concepts that are used are decisive in highlighting the moral significance, and thus determine, at least in part, what values are at stake, what attitudes are fitting, what principles ought to govern action in particular occasions, and what means of action are appropriate. Insofar as the symbols and concepts used are a part of the Christian religious heritage, their usage suggests that ethics might be Christian in a limited but distinctive way.

Indeed, the use of Christian symbols and concepts in this way has been so much a part of the stock-in-trade, the conventional wisdom, of a large part of Protestant theological ethics that a formal articulation of the process has seldom been noted. Insofar as theologians have had great confidence in the heuristic power of Christian symbols and concepts, they have consciously stated, or quietly assumed, that their use is the only way to comprehend what is "really" happening in a particular sequence of events, what the "true," or the "ultimate," significance of circumstances is, what are the most decisive forces or factors involved. For example, there have been many theologians who would use the term sin to point to the suspicion of human corruption that was present in the perception of my companion in New York. This term, often articulated as a concept, is a part of their framework for analysis and understanding of what is occurring in events and relations. It enables them to "see" things in a different light; it shapes their interpretations of what is going on, and thus it determines in part what is of moral significance. Or, for another example, during periods of great social unrest and upheaval in Western society such as the sixteenth century, there have been religious leaders who interpreted the significance of these events as signs of the return of Christ, as the catastrophic ending of an old order and an old era, and the dawning of a new order and a new age of righteousness. They believed they saw a "deeper" significance to peasants' revolts and to ecclesiastical revolutions than others had the eyes to see. The significance that they perceived and the symbols that both guided their perceptions and expressed them were influential in determining how they responded to the event. Radical reformers like Thomas Münzer encouraged revolt; the more conservative reformer Martin Luther wrote a famous piece that in the end condemns the peasants.

That there are serious intellectual problems in this use of concepts and symbols is seen in the fact that the same event, or the same set of circumstances, can be interpreted very differently by different theologians. The third decade of the sixteenth century in Germany is only one example of this. Contemporary social upheavals provide another example. The dominant theological symbol used in our time for interpreting the significance of the struggles of oppressed minorities in the United States and of the poor throughout the world is "liberation."[1] While there are no prominent writers who use the more apocalyptic imagery that sixteenth-century Continental writers and seventeenth-century English radicals used—seeing in the event of social upheaval the return of Christ, for example—other religious symbols and theological concepts do lead to a positive evaluation of these movements. The terms crucifixion and resurrection have been used; the old order is going through the death agonies, and it must be crucified so that out of its death a new order can be "resurrected."[2] Or, the event of the exodus in the ancient history of the Hebrew people has been used as a symbol of God's liberating activity, leading the oppressed out of bondage and into liberty.[3] Or, a concept of God's activity as "humanizing" activity is articulated in such a way that the events of social upheaval can be interpreted as occasions in which God's humanizing work is being done in the world.[4] Various symbols and concepts that relate to liberation are used to designate the ultimate religious *and moral* significance of events; an imperative follows, namely, that Christians should support the efforts of the poor and the oppressed. The same social movements and events are seen to be more ambiguous in their moral dimensions and to evoke a more ambivalent or cautionary response by other theologians. Pope Paul's encyclical *On the Development of Peoples* is an example. In paragraphs 29–32, he states that many peoples are suffering grave injustices that require rectification. The concept of justice, which has theological warrants developed through a theology of creation and of natural law, is used to evaluate the circumstances. In these circumstances it appears that recourse to violence is a morally licit means of action. The pope warns, however, that the consequences of a violent revolution might be worse than the present injustice, and he appeals to a notion of equilibrium; too radical a response upsets a necessary equilibrium in society. The consequences of the weight given to equilibrium in the process of social interpretation leads to greater caution in responding to revolutionary forces than do various religious symbols of liberation.[5]

The responses of churches and theologians to the rise of German nationalism under the rule of the Nazis will be long studied for various reasons. Two such responses suffice to make clear that the same sequence of events and the ideology that supported it were assessed differently in part because of the theological concepts that were used. From the standpoint of Reinhold Niebuhr, for example, what was occurring in Germany was an occasion of the collective immorality that manifests itself in the sinful pride of nations. It was a case of fanatic idolatry. This evil, coupling a mythology of Aryan superiority with growing military power, had to be resisted. The concepts of idolatry and sin, and particularly of pride, were used to interpret what was going on in such a way that its demonic significance was profoundly exposed. There were, however, some German Protestant theologians who during the same period were using the concept of *Das Volk* as an order of creation to articulate the religious and moral significance of the same German nationalism.[6] That concept, obviously, with its consequences appealed for support of German nationalism on the part of Christians. Intensified consciousness of national unity and identity was judged to be healthy; it was the historical actualization of an order of creation.

There are basically two intellectual difficulties in this use of religious symbols and theological concepts; the second may, indeed, be only a particular instance of the first. The first, in question form is, what authorizes or justifies this use of religious symbols and concepts at all? The second is, by what criteria can theologians and churches determine which symbols and which concepts *ought* to be used to interpret the events and circumstances to which they are called to respond? Each question opens vast expanses of theological methods: both the analysis made here and the constructive proposals are sketchy.

The Authority of Religious Symbols and Concepts

What authorizes or justifies this interpretative use of religious symbols and theological concepts at all? For some, religious symbols and concepts have authority insofar as they are biblical in origin or in content. They are part of "revelation." The interpretations of what "revealed in scripture" means are many; and I shall indicate only two uses of the notion. One is a positivistic verbal meaning that would be affirmed only by a fundamentalist. This is important to note because a significant amount of Protestant fundamentalist preaching engages in self-styled "prophecy," that is, the prediction of future events on the basis of an interpretation of present circumstances in the light of biblical narratives or mythological symbols. The homiletical move is usually an analogical one, or at least one of citing presumed similiarities between events of our time and those that Daniel or the author of the Apocalypse seemed to have in mind. The professed warrant for this sort of prophecy is the literal inspiration of the biblical texts; "It says in the Bible..." seems to be sufficient. But the imaginative and rhetorical gifts of the preacher are obviously necessary to make the move from a text to what is now happening and to what is likely to happen. How such a preacher selects his texts raises our second question, that of criteria. For reasons not distinctive enough to mention, the fundamentalist version of authority is rejected.

More sophisticated and more persuasive is a view that defends biblical revelation in more historical, dynamic, and existential terms. The narratives of scripture are records of events in and through which God discloses his activity; he discloses something of himself, of his relation to the world, and of the reality of the world itself. What authorizes the use of biblical symbols and concepts is not the fact that they can be found in the book, but that in the records of that book there is a relatively clear and accurate perception of what is most significant (or in the terms of some theologians, what is most real) about human life and human action. What makes it most significant is that in those records there is an interpretation of the relations of nature, human events, and persons to the *ultimate* power that stands over against them. The dimensions that are disclosed are not only political (for example, Israel's role in the military struggles for hegemony in the ancient Near Eastern circumstances), not only economic (for example, the responsibilities that the early Pauline congregations assumed for the support of the congregation in Jerusalem) and not only social (for example, the ordering of relations between married persons at various times and places in the accounts recorded). Rather, by viewing these and other dimensions of experience in relation to the ultimate power, to God, a special significance (or for some theologians, the *real* significance) of these dimensions is articulated.[7] Thus the authority of the symbols and concepts lies in their powers to disclose dimensions of events, of circumstances, and of persons that might not be perceived by other beliefs, other symbols, other concepts.

This kind of authority necessarily contains an element of "subjectivity"; there are bound to be many persons in modern pluralistic cultures who do not perceive the significance that a theological interpretation cites. While certain empirical evidences might be cited by the theologian to provide backing for his interpretation, and while persons might even be persuaded of the validity of the theologian's perceptive insight, the value that the symbols have subjectively for the theologian might escape his sympathetic secular colleagues. A theologian's interpretation of events might yield insight into various forces that are at work historically such as Reinhold Niebuhr's did; to the nonreligious person the power of beliefs and concepts that yield this insight are valued in terms of their disclosure of aspects or dimensions of what is going on in the world. If theological concepts yield no such insight they are of no value, they have no authority for a person. The religious person who uses these concepts often has a more complex pattern of authorization. Symbols and concepts have authority not only because they enable the theologian to perceive aspects and dimensions of circumstances but also because they are confirmed in the religious dimensions of his experience. They arise out of the religious dimensions of his consciousness as well as out of his participation in and observation of what is occurring in events. Indeed, the theologian is wont to claim that the interpretative power of the concepts and symbols is intrinsically related to their more distinctively religious dimensions. In some sense, and often in *what* sense is vague, the theologian affirms that his concepts and symbols used in the interpretation of events have more than heuristic value, and what heuristic value they have is grounded in their significance as articulations of the experience of the reality of God and of life before God.

The impact of Reinhold Niebuhr on some statesmen and political philosophers has been noted frequently and provides a useful example for analysis. "Atheists for Niebuhr" provides a useful caption. Niebuhr's criticisms of American democratic liberalism as it was both preached and practiced in the second quarter of this century were persuasive to many who were only marginally interested in the theological concepts that provided an underpinning for his insightful social and political analyses, as Arthur Schlesinger, Jr., demonstrates by his account of Niebuhr's role in American political thought and life.[8] To be an atheist for Niebuhr, if this meant that a reader could agree with his analysis of the significance of events and circumstances while rejecting his theological concepts and their foundations, seems to imply that his theology was accidental to his interpretative and evaluative powers. It was dispensable baggage. Or if the theology was important, its import resided in its biographical function; it could be claimed that it was necessary for Niebuhr personally, but not necessary for others. Niebuhr apparently did not evangelize his political and philosophical allies, and thus he appears to concede at least the point that for others the theology was not necessary, or at least the traditional Christian concepts and symbols that he used to articulate it—agape as self-sacrificial love, sin and its forms, the cross—were not necessary conditions for the appreciation of the insights. Whether Niebuhr could have come to these insights without the religious dimensions of his life and thought is an unanswerable speculative question. Yet the proposal that in his most influential years Niebuhr found powerful meanings of the many aspects of human life disclosed in the biblical accounts and in subsequently developed theological concepts is surely warranted. There was, for him, a confirmation in experiece of the truths perceived in religious concepts and symbols. And the interpretation of social and political life in the light of these yielded an account which in turn shaped the statement of the fundamental moral issues and predisposed certain responses to them in terms of both ends to be sought and means to be used.

Of equal interest for purposes of our analysis are two articles by H. Richard Niebuhr,[9] whose publications of an interpretative mode were all too few indeed. In the midst of World War II, Niebuhr dicussed God's action in the events that occupied attention at that time. From these articles one can infer that his experience of the reality of God was one of God's presence mediated through events, God's action in and through human actions and historical circumstances. He wrote that "it is a sign of returning health when God rather than the self or the enemy is seen to be the central figure in the great tragedy of war and when the question 'What must I do?' is preceded by the question 'What is God doing?' To attend to God's action is to be on the way to that constructive understanding and constructive human reaction which the prophets initiated."[10] These articles do not deal with the idea of revelation that underlies them[11] but it clearly involves a confirmation in the experience of the believer that his symbols and concepts, though historically conditioned, enable him to understand (though seeing through a glass darkly) what God is doing in the war. There is nothing facile or absolutely certain about this interpretation; it comes out of earnest struggle and reflection. But it does provide a "theory of the events in which he is participating,"[12] an interpretation that directs human action. The two symbols of judgment and crucifixion, then, provide an interpretation of the significance of the war, which in turn guides attitudes and actions.

To see how this is done does not resolve head-on the issue of the authority of the symbols but demonstrates how they are used when they are confirmed in religious faith. Judgment for Christians, for example, cannot be separated from redemption, "the harshness of God is not antagonistic to his love but subordinate to it," the "divine 'penology' is reconstructive and not vindictive in its nature." What does this aspect of "judgment" disclose about the war? Christians cannot interpret God's action in the war as a judgment of vengeance; rather, the war is a chastening punishment that can change the character of those who produced its destructive acts. Also, since the suffering of war descends primarily on the innocent rather than the unjust, on the simple people rather than the powerful leaders of nation, war is crucifixion. Using this, "Christians know that the justice of God is not only a redemptive justice in which suffering is used in service of remaking but it is also vicarious in its method so that the suffering of innocence is used for the remaking of the guilty." Further, in the light of God's judgment "there can be no contention before him about the relative rightness or wrongness of the various groups involved." This means that if Hitler is the rod of God's anger, he is not justified for he does not intend what God intends; if the Allies are the instruments of God's judgment on Hitler, they are not thereby justified.[13]

H. Richard Niebuhr draws from this "certain consequences for human action." We are not to be preoccupied with our rightness or wrongness, with self-justification, but with our duty in view of what God is doing. This involves "resistance to those who are abusing our neighbors" whether or not our neighbors are better than those abusing them. We are to abandon all "self-defensiveness" and all "self-aggrandizement" and see that there is a judgment on our nation which "has demonstrated its profound preoccupation with its own prosperity, safety and righteousness, so that in its withdrawal from international political responsibilities, in its tariff, monetary and neutrality legislation it has acted always with a single eye to its own interests rather than those of its neighbors in the commonwealth of nations." To make war under God's judgment is to do so as those "who will not withdraw when their own interests are no longer apparently imperiled while their weaker neighbors remain in danger," as those who "accept continuous never ending responsibilities for their neighbors." "It is also to wage war in such a way that a decent—a just endurable if not a just and durable—peace can come out of it." Under God's judgment we never demonize the enemy, "as though he were too depraved for redemption or for restoration to full rights in the human community." It is to see a time of judgment as a time of redemption, to "look in the midst of tragedy for the emergence of a better order."[14]

This summary does not do full justice to the subtlety and the religious eloquence of Niebuhr's article. It does, however, illustrate our contention that the use of religious symbols like judgment and crucifixion to interpret the significance of an event like war predisposes the religious community to certain attitudes and to a general course of action. It is apparent in these articles that for Niebuhr, the *Christian community* ought to seek to interpret events in the light of God's action, for God's action is decisive in determining the possibilities for faithful human action. Also, Niebuhr had confidence that for Christians these symbols and concepts disclose the sorts of action to be expected of

God in these events. God is judging all participating nations in the war; war is a crucifixion of the innocent. The significance of the events lies, for the religious community, in what God is doing in them. But there is confidence that this significance is universal; it goes beyond those who use these symbols. Something very fundamental about these events is "revealed" through the interpretation. Thus while Christians have particular symbols, the symbols disclose what is universally significant both about God and about events. War is "at least very much like the crucifixion." The cross, that most distinctive of Christian symbols, yields insight not only into the suffering of the innocent but also into the possible benefits from it; it discloses God's "moral earnestness" and God's graciousness. The cross does not impose a new law on men, but restrains them from claiming a righteousness of their own and from vengeance and enables men to act in hope and in reliance on God's graciousness.

Some distance from these illustrations is now needed to examine what sorts of authorization the use of religious symbols and theological concepts can have for interpretating the significance of circumstances and events. We noted and swiftly dismissed a literalistic, fundamentalistic authority. We noted that the general sort of authority illustrated by both of the Niebuhrs introduced an element of subjectivity, of confirmation in the experience of the person who used them. Some more refined distinctions among the sorts of authority need to be made. Distinctively different from the literalistic, fundamentalistic authority is one that gives exclusive authority to scripture because it was in the events (not just the words) recounted there that God freely chose to disclose himself to man. Scripture is the locus of human knowledge of God because such knowledge is not possible apart from God's free choice to reveal himself; and he made that choice (and thus bound himself) in relation to the events and persons recorded in the Bible. What are there disclosed are the "real" dimensions of God, of man, and of history.[15] What authorizes the use of symbols and concepts is not the location of the words (that is, in the Bible) as in fundamentalism, but God's decision to reveal what is "real" through the events there recorded. The theologian is to function as the faithful interpreter of the real that is revealed, and the Bible is his text for that. A rein on subjectivity is presumed, for the revelation is "objectively" given in scriptures. In a sense, then, if one can argue that his interpretation is in accord with "the real" disclosed in scripture, it is accurate.

At the opposite extreme from this position would be a very skeptical one, namely, that religious symbols and theological concepts have authority only for those who are socialized in a community that already assumes they are authorized. In addition, perhaps, this community is judged to be esoteric; its symbols and concepts are so private that they disclose nothing about human events that is experienced by other persons.

No sophisticated theologian would accept this view, not even those for whom biblical authority is exclusive, for on one basis or another the Christian community claims that its symbols and concepts do have universal significance. That claim, however, contains a problem. If what the symbols and concepts yield in the interpretation of events is something universally significant about them, the failure of others to perceive that significance counts against the claim to universality. If, for example, the use of the symbol of the cross to interpret a war discloses not only that it is the innocent who suffer most (a judgment that is susceptible to some empirical verification) but also that the suffering of the innocent can work vicariously for the benefit of the guilty and for all men (by creating the occasion for repentance and for an emandation of human affairs which would seek to prohibit the recurrence of such events), is that interpretation of the significance of war universally persuasive? Would the fact that repentance and turning from the ways of war is ephemeral count against the use of the symbol of the cross? Or, is what is disclosed more a theological point, namely, that God is gracious, and in his grace has created the conditions under which some benefits can emerge from even the greatest evil of the deaths of the innocent? If the answer is affirmative to this last question, does that not also appeal to the possibilities of an experiential confirmation on the part of those who do not use that symbol? I believe that it does.

This suggests a range of authority that I believe is capable of defense and that can be distinguished from the stronger claims for biblical authority and the weaker claims that the accusation of a mere social authority seem to merit. Religious persons experience the reality of God in and through experiences that at the same time are experiences of something else. Out of participation in many events and diverse circumstances have come the articulation of symbols and concepts which always have a double reference. On the one hand, they refer to the significance of the events and circumstances in the light of the experience of God; on the other hand, they refer to the experience of the ultimate power (and thus the articulation of this) in the light of the events and circumstances. The contemporary Christian community is in part continuous with the biblical communities and with the post-biblical church. There is a continuity of experience in which events are interpreted in the light of symbols and concepts that have come from previous experience; there is a continuing process of resymbolizing and reconceptualizing the reality of God and his relations to creation and history in the light of new experiences. As a result of this ongoing process, the authority of religious symbols and theological concepts for use in interpreting the significance of circumstances can never be an absolutely fixed authority; it always has a subjective aspect for individuals and communities. If the use of specific symbols does not confirm this power to disclose something of profound significance in circumstances and events, their authority (at least for the moment) is diminished. Other specific religious symbols in the tradition might be utilized, or nontraditional symbols and concepts might be chosen. Since the symbols and concepts presumably aid in disclosing more than an esoteric and private significance, the failure to evoke comprehension if not assent by nonreligious persons involved in the same events signals serious problems. The problems can be of many sorts: failure of communication by the interpreter, inept selection of symbols and concepts, the ossification of the traditional symbols, the difficulties of any sort of persuasive interpretation under the condition of competing symbols and concepts that refer to the same or to similar dimensions of experience. If a religious or theological interpretation of the significance of events does not render an account that is at least intelligible (if not convincing) to persons outside the religious circle, it obviously needs to be reconsidered. Yet the need for reconsideration does not immediately imply that the concepts or symbols must be abandoned, for they have been confirmed by the experience of the religious community and they refer not only to human events, but to the experience of the perduring power that stands over against us.

To Christians and others the looseness of the claims I have made may be regrettable. A test that would require greater precision is conceivable—for example, further analysis of the intelligibility and the persuasiveness of H. Richard Niebuhr's use of the symbol of the cross to interpret the significance of World War II. Such a test cannot be developed here; the looseness or weakness of my claims will have to remain. But at least a descriptive conclusion is warranted: religious symbols and theological concepts are used to interpret the significance of circumstances and events in which human action is required. The significance that is elucidated determines in part what values are at stake, what moral attitudes are fitting, what principles and intentions are applicable, and perhaps also what means ought to be used. The justification for using religious symbols and concepts is that, emerging as they do out of the religious dimensions of human experience, they enable the interpreter and others to perceive profoundly important dimensions, characteristics, and meanings in what is occurring. These dimensions are intrinsically related to the perceptions of the reality of God. The use of certain Christian symbols might lead to an interpretation of the significance of certain events in such a way that what is perceived is "colored" by the symbols used. There might be something distinctively Christian in the understanding of war in the light of the cross, though what is disclosed is appropriate because it is universally significant and not just because it was "seen" through the use of that symbol. In this circumspect way, ethical reflection might be distinctively Christian.

Criteria for the Selection of Symbols and Concepts

If my companion at the bar used notions of honesty and fairness that were central in his understanding of the significance of what was occurring in the series of personal interactions on that occasion, he could justify their selection by reference to their appropriateness to the events. No one asked him why he chose the notions he did from a series of important ones. In chapter 4 I simulated a conversation between us that might get at some more general reasons for his interest in honesty and fairness, but these supporting reasons, at least as stated there, would not provide sufficient grounds for selecting honesty. Other terms or notions could be supported for the same reasons. Honesty and fairness appeared on the face of it to be applicable to evaluating the significance of those incidents; that was reason enough for their apparent primacy. It is not that simple with religious symbols and with theological concepts.

I indicated that different theologians sometimes chose different concepts or symbols to expound the significance of the same events, with the result that the significance that one perceives is opposed to what another perceives. German nationalism in the decade of the 1930s was interpreted as an evil force, for it was understood in relation to corporate pride and idolatry by some; it was interpreted by others as a healthy phenomenon because it seemed to be the fulfillment of the function of *Das Volk*, an order of creation. In that case, it appears that the circumstances to which theologians are responding are not sufficient to determine what symbols and concepts are appropriate to them. When the choice of concepts is decisive in judging the moral worth of what is going on, and two different concepts lead to opposing evaluations, the problem is of sufficient magnitude to make many sensitive and rational persons despair of religion and theology altogether. "You can prove anything from the Bible," the old comment goes. Religious symbols and theological concepts within the Christian tradition are sufficiently numerous and varied that one can be found to support almost any significance one perceives in events. That this is the case can be illustrated from a conversation I had with a South African theologian in which I was expounding how persons used biblical analogies to contemporary events to support their causes. I cited the use of the exodus event to understand the meaning of social liberation movements and to lend biblical authority to them.[16] His response illustrated the issue under discussion then, and now. He indicated that in the nineteenth century Dutch Calvinists in South Africa used the conquest of the land of Canaan to support their expansion into the lands of the black tribes. Whether the exodus or the conquest is the appropriate symbol depends not on biblical authority in a crude sense but on the prior identification of the oppressed or of the conquerors as God's special "elect." What adds to the ambiguity is that the oppressed who were liberated subsequently became the conquerors. Our question, then, is what criteria control, and ought to control, the selection of religious symbols and theological concepts that are to be used to interpret the significance of circumstances and events? What principles determine the selection, and how are the selected symbols used?[17] Five principles will be cited, and the two that seem most justifiable will be discussed at some length; indeed the final one which I shall support is developed from these two.

The first is one that is fundamentally dishonest: it is that whatever symbols and concepts have an effective force in persuasive rhetoric, these are the appropriate ones to use. Thus if a preacher is seeking support from a group of Bible-believing pious Christians for his interpretation of a conflict he perceives between the forces of evil ("materialism," "communism," "sexual freedom") and the forces of righteousness, he can evoke support for his opinion by interpreting the conflict in the symbols to which such people respond. He can draw an analogy between the present conflict that he perceives and the Battle of Armageddon, for example, and if he persuades his hearers that his identifications of the analogues is proper, he has enhanced the authority of his opinion. Perhaps this is done in good faith, and thus is not dishonest. There is, however, a sufficient amount of chauvinistic propaganda in some "fundamentalist" preaching to evoke a skeptical raising of an eyebrow. One can choose religious symbols for their rhetorical effectiveness to gain support for an interpretation that is governed more basically by other concepts and beliefs.

The second is honest but insufficiently critical. It is that the circumstances or events to be interpreted determine (via an intuitive sense) what symbols or concepts are appropriate. The lack of critical justification might not make the selection wrong. For example, in H. Richard Niebuhr's articles on war, he does not engage in a defense of his selection of the judgment of God and of crucifixion as the fitting symbols for interpreting what God was doing in those events. Nor would it occur to most readers to raise the question. Involvement in war, for the morally earnest religious community, seems to suggest their appropriateness. Some other symbols are patently out of order; the involvement in suffering of the innocents does not suggest that resurrection or other symbols of triumph are appropriate. The costliness (in many dimensions) of war suggests divine judgment more than it does the coming of God's Kingdom. Niebuhr, however, specifically rejects certain plausible symbols, like God's vengeful action to destroy the evil doers; in doing so he cites theological reasons. The idea that God is acting in vengeance is illicit, even though there are plausible analogies to World War II in scripture which suggest that God may be seeking vengeance in wars. It is illicit because of a theological generalization, namely, that God's action is gracious and redeeming, and this precludes vengeance. But this points to another criterion for selection; it is noted here, however, to indicate that while the circumstances of a highly destructive war lend a *prima facie* plausibility to the choice of the symbols of judgment and crucifixion, other criteria than appropriateness to the events under scrutiny are probably always involved in the selection and use of symbols.

A third criterion is also more honest that the first, but also insufficiently critical. It can be stated as follows: Whatever symbols and concepts elaborate, clarify, and justify one's already formed moral opinion (and this may be informed by a religious outlook) can be used. In my judgment many religious thinkers who implicitly use this criterion are not conscious of the difficulty involved. The main problem is that the interpreter appears to have made an independent (from theology) moral assessment of the circumstances and events and then selected among the religious symbols available those which confirm this assessment, those that are most effective in interpreting the events so as to confirm theologically the interpreter's independent moral assessment. This may be a pseudo-difficulty, but only if a rationale can be given to bring together the moral and theological assessments. Before pointing to such a rationale, however, the difficulty needs further illustration.

Without charging particular authors with not recognizing this difficulty, we can state hypothetically what is involved. (I believe, obviously, that the charge can be made against particular texts.) We live in a period of history when the poor and ethnic minorities in many parts of the world are seeking freedom from oppression. The religious and moral sympathies of many serious Christians are clearly with the oppressed. Let us bracket for a moment very plausible reasons for this, namely, that the gospel is for the poor, or God wills liberation. Certain events recorded in the biblical accounts, and certain religious symbols, are selected to elaborate, clarify, and justify this sympathy, to interpret the significance of some contemporary events, and to yield by inference some general action-guiding principles. The exodus of the Hebrew people from their bondage to the powerful Egyptians seems to be historically analogous to the contemporary movements as I have previously noted. Clarification is needed about why the exodus is such a significant symbol. One criterion would be that under scrutiny here, namely, that many Christians have a moral conviction about the need to free persons from poverty and social oppression; therefore they select the exodus as an interpretive symbol. It lends religious authority to their moral opinion, for God was clearly on the side of the Hebrew people according to the account. The question I have previously suggested is relevant here: why not select the conquest of Canaan which apparently had equal approval of the Divinity? Basically, the first answer to that is a moral one; liberation is morally good, conquest is morally bad. If that is the only answer, the response is insufficiently critical from a theological point of view. What is required to make it more sufficient is a theological argument, to wit, that liberation is more consistent with the Christian experience of God than is conquest and suppression. As H. Richard Niebuhr used a more general theological affirmation to rule vengeful activity out of God's action in war, so those who use the exodus symbol have to use a more general theological affirmation to support the primacy of liberation, and thus support the validity of the exodus analogy. They would have to marshal an argument that the exodus experience discloses something more real about God's purposes than does the conquest of Canaan; or, that the exodus event is confirmed by subsequent "revelatory" events in a way that the conquest is not; or, that on the basis of a more systematic Christian theology there is warrant for selecting the exodus over the conquest. Again, this points ahead to another criterion.

The formal point could be made with reference to other symbols. Does, for example, the breakdown of old forms of social order in various parts of the world with which many morally sensitive religious people are in sympathy, give warrant for the use of the symbols of crucifixion and resurrection to interpret the significance of these events? Alternative justifications for their use might be two. One is that the crucifixion and resurrection of Jesus discloses what is "most real" about historical processes, and thus can be used to interpret the "real" significance of what is occurring. A second might be that the crucifixion and resurrection of Jesus disclose God's will for what *ought* to go on in history, and thus these are the proper symbols to use to interpret events in order to see what persons ought to be doing. Both of these bristle with problems if analogical thinking is done with care. In first-century Palestine it was not the oppressive Roman governor who was nailed to the cross but the innocent man, or (as in the light of our times, New Testament exegetes are more prone to stress) the protester against oppression.[18] In the use of the analogy, who, or what contemporary group is to be "crucified"? Are present circumstances sufficiently similar to those of first-century Palestine to warrant the analogy? How precisely would "resurrection" have to be identified to make it a clear symbol? This suggests the sorts of questions that could be asked.[19]

The basic point to be stressed is that if a prior moral opinion is the criterion for the selection of symbols and concepts to interpret the significance of events, then to make that *theologically* and *religiously* legitimate a theological basis for that moral opinion must be articulated. If it is not, then religious symbols and concepts are the subordinate servants of moral opinions. I believe, as other parts of this book have sought to claim, that such an outcome is not true to the experience of God's reality in the Christian community.

A fourth criterion is that the concepts and symbols are to be selected in accordance with the ordering of doctrines in a rigorous theological system. The accent, for our purposes, is on a *rigorous* theological system, for as I shall develop the fifth criterion, an appeal will be made to theology, but in a less tightly systematic form.

Highly systematic theologies are both admirably helpful and questionably oversimplified. To have a rigorous theological system, some crucial judgment is determinative of all that is conceptually ordered. Or there may be a few judgments well correlated with each other that are decisive. For example, theologians have taken a specific Christian doctrine to be the primary one and thus ordered other doctrines in relation to this one. Currently the theological world of Christianity is being exposed to both European and American efforts to make eschatology the principal motif of theology.[20] The formal process for making such a claim to primacy in traditional academic theology is to show the insufficiencies of other theological positions that have made other doctrines primary, or that have at least failed to perceive the primacy of eschatology. These insufficiencies are judged on the basis of several different appeals: one is usually a reexamination of biblical evidences and a marshaling of exegesis to show why hope or eschatology is central to the scriptural message. Another is usually an appeal to some philosophical themes; in the case of our example they may be neo-Hegelian or neo-Marxist ones. If the systematizer wishes the biblical authority to be final, he must argue that his selected or constructed philosophical pattern is implicit in scripture, or is most consistent with scripture. Other theologians might take other doctrinal motifs to be central and engage in a similiar process. Or, theologians might judge a particular metaphysician or ontological thinker to be correct—for example, Alfred North Whitehead—and organize a "process theology" out of such a view. If they desire also to be "Christian" theologians, they must find a way to correlate certain historic Christian themes with this philosophy.[21]

The crucial judgments of the theologian are established and defended. They may be a combination of methodological and doctrinal judgments. Some epistemological assumptions are made, for example, that determine where on a continuum between "natural" theology and a highly "confessional" theology the position is located. Some doctrinal judgments are made, and would be correlated with the epistemological assumption; for example, Christology is judged to be the crucial doctrine in Barth's highly confessional theology. From such judgments a more or less rigorously ordered system of doctrines is established.

This sketch of the way systematic theologians work will have to suffice; for our purposes it is important to note that once a system is highly ordered, there are grounds for judging which theological concepts ought to have primacy in the interpretation of the significance of events and circumstances. The selection is authorized by the ordering of theological principles and doctrines within the system. If eschatology is theologically established to be what Christianity is all about, then a concept of eschatology ought to be the primary one in interpreting contemporary events. What is disclosed by such an interpretation, then, is proper because it comes from the use of the proper concept or symbol.

This is both beneficial and problematically simple. It is beneficial because it lends itself to clarity (in principle, though not always in fact). A clear answer can be given to the question, why does a theologian use hope, for instance, as the basic symbol for interpreting the significance of contemporary events? The answer, because hope is central to the Christian message, and the doctrine of hope is the key to Christian theology. As we have seen, how that clear answer is itself defended might be very complex indeed.

The clarity and simplicity of this way of working are precisely what make it questionable. What doctrine is to be primary is harder to establish than some theologians appear to believe; the ongoing literature of theology is the story of the differences in judgments on this matter. More important for our account is that a rigorous systematic ordering of doctrines seems to falsify the richness and complexity of the Christian experience of God's reality. God is the God of the future, yes; God is also the God of the past and the present. Thus symbols and concepts that take past and present seriously are as worthy of use as those that take the future seriously. Man is a sinner, yes; but a theology that accents the importance of this too heavily loses sight of the powers of renewal and possibility that are a part of the reality of God in

relation to events and persons. God is the reconciler and redeemer, yes; but without taking into account his creative activity a
dimension of human experience of him is absent.

The simplification that warrants the use of one symbol or
concept, or that too rigidly orders the priority of symbols and
concepts, has consequences for the interpretation of the significance of events. For example, an interpretation in the light of a
doctrine of hope without qualification by a doctrine of sin and
moral evil can lead to a perception that blinds Christians to the
intransigencies of the powers that resist modification of the
course of events in the direction of what is beneficial to the human
community. This has consequences for the attitudes toward
events that are shaped, and for the courses of action that might be
judged to be proper.

A clear statement of a fifth criterion will follow from what I
believe must be taken into account in its formation. That there
must be some ordering principles which give guidance to the
selection of symbols I have intimated in the discussions of the
second and third criteria. A sense of appropriateness based on an
intuition is insufficient, and a moral criterion that is not given
some theological defense violates the purpose of a theological
enterprise. The problems of an excessively rigorous theological
system I have sought to indicate in the discussion of the fourth
criterion. These criticisms set boundaries within which a criterion
(and it must be complex) I would defend must be developed. It
must also be developed in relation to some basic thrusts of earlier
chapters in this book.

My basic assumption is that the experience of God's reality
within the context of the Christian community and tradition is
multidimensional. This has been elucidated most fully in chapter
4. Thus any articulation of that experience, any intelligible
account of it, must take into account the various aspects of God's
relation to man that are present. This builds in a pluralism that is
both problematic and beneficial. It is problematic because the
dimensions of experience do not necessarily fall into a neat and
harmonious whole, at least on first examination. To experience
God as the judge of moral disorder in the social sphere is not
immediately harmonious with experiencing him as the reconciler

and redeemer of life. To acknowledge radical dependence on God is on the face of it abrasive against acknowledging humans to be agents with capacities for giving direction to events. Christian theology has always recognized this difficulty; its trinitarian and other vocabularies have been developed in the effort to articulate the plurality of the dimensions of human experience of God. The task of the theologian is to give some order to these dimensions, which is by inference to give some order to the perceptions of the ultimate power. Yet, as I have attempted to show, an excessively systematic order violates the richness of the primal experience. The problem that plurality creates for the interpretation of the significance of circumstances is that different concepts and symbols exist which are pertinent to the circumstances under discussion. It is precisely the problem of this section. The benefits of that plurality are that it is more accurate with reference to the religious dimensions of experience. In its context there is immediate resistance to excessive simplification.

To provide some guidance in selection, some judgments must be made, and they need to be theological. How they are related to morality is a matter deferred for the moment. To make a judgment in the light of the basic thrust of this book requires an examination of the following question: are there occasions in the history of the biblically informed communities that seem to warrant theological generalization and judgment on certain decisive issues? To make a full defense of my answer would require a full historical and theological treatise; it must suffice to affirm that there are such occasions. They are those which lead to expressions of the priority of the beneficence of the ultimate power. Grace is prior to nature and nature is a gift of grace. Gospel is prior to law, and the law is a form of the gospel. Forgiveness is prior to sin, and restoration and reconciliation are prior to brokenness and estrangement. The ultimate power seeks the well-being of creation, and creates the conditions in which there are possibilities to achieve a measure of well-being even in catastrophies, social upheavals, and personal despair, even in suffering, sin, and death. I dare to affirm that these phrases point to the fundamental intention of the ultimate power. The experience out of which they come is that of the Jewish people who are the spiritual ancestors and current relatives of the

Christian community. It is the experience of the Christian community's response to Jesus Christ and his disclosing power. It is the experience articulated in numerous theologies through the history of Christian thought.

This affirmation of God's intentionality includes moral aspects; the well-being intended includes the moral well-being of the human community. Other aspects of well-being are present, such as "salvation" and "healthiness"; the relations of these to moral well-being is not our concern here. The inclusion of moral well-being sustains the legitimacy of the use of religious symbols and theological concepts to evaluate the moral significance of events. It also suggests the possibility of formulating some criteria for the selection of concepts and symbols under particular circumstances. In part the choice of symbols and concepts will be made according to their efficacy in clarifying the moral and human values that are at stake on particular personal and historic social occasions. Thus appropriateness to the circumstances is also a legitimate appeal to make. But the choice will also be made with reference to a critical conceptualization and ordering of theological concepts and religious symbols. Other symbols will be used within the governing context of the priority of grace over nature, gospel over law, forgiveness over wrath, reconciliaton over estrangement, restoration over brokenness, liberation over bondage, and so on.

The critical task involves other sets of judgments. Since biblical symbols and theological concepts frequently refer to both moral and nonmoral aspects of human ends and divine purposes, the sophisticated interpreter of events needs to develop certain specifically ethical correlates of these terms. The notion that men are to do all things to the glory of God, for example, is not simply a moral command. God is glorified in religious communities by praising him, singing hymns, offering prayers of thanksgiving, celebrating his presence in the world "with joy and thanksgiving." Yet certain ethical inferences can be made from the admonition to glorify God. What patterns of human institutional relations would "show forth the glory of God"? If God is glorified when his purposes for creation are on occasion fulfilled, and if these purposes include moral well-being, and moral values, then an ordering of society which realizes what the religious community perceives God to value is one that shows his glory, or glorifies him. From the experience of the religious community (and from broader human experience) we know something of the social conditions that are in accord with the intention of the ultimate power. God values justice; justice is an indispensable condition for social and individual well-being. There are religious grounds for using a concept of justice to interpret and evaluate social, political, and economic life. Social orders which are gross violations of distributive justice do not show forth the glory of God.

The use of the symbol of liberation is frequent in current Christian interpretations, and its inclusiveness is clear from the range and dimensions of experiences it refers to. Where persons are being liberated from mores and taboos that have suppressed their natural sexual impulses, there is liberation. Many Christians see this as in accord with God's purposes. Other socially enforced restrictions on the rights of groups are undergoing alteration— women, ethnic minorities, nations under political and economic domination of foreign powers, and the like. There, too, God is judged by many Christians to be at work. Biblical warrants can be given for this judgment; the gospel sets men free, for example. The value that liberation has for Christians authorized its use as a symbol (often it is not specified clearly as a concept should be) for interpreting the significance of events; it is the basis for an evaluative description of what is going on. But its evocative power requires supplementation by more rigorously defined concepts to give a more detailed assessment of certain circumstances, and to provide action-guiding principles. Again the principle of distributive justice is pertinent. The specification of a formal principle of distributive justice is required by the use of the symbol of liberation. That a concept of justice requires material specification (for example, equal treatment according to ascribed status, to merit, or to need) is clear. I would argue that a *pressure toward* need is consistent with Christian religious convictions, but that is not my purpose here. What is important to note is that certain ethical concepts have theological warrants which legitimate their priority in the evaluation of events and circumstances.

Finally, before a more systematic formulation of a fifth criterion is made, the assumption that this process of interpretation takes place under changing historical, social, and personal conditions needs to be acknowledged. This rules out a fixed ordering of symbols derived from an eternal and immutable revelation of nature that can be rationalistically used to assess what is equally eternally and immutably of moral significance in all particular human events and circumstances. On the contrary, the interpretation is a process going on with a plurality of symbols and concepts in changing events and circumstances, and with interpreters who reflect their own historic periods, social circumstances, and individual experiences. This "relativism" is not boundless, for within plurality and change there can be an important but finally provisional ordering of symbols and concepts; the process takes place in a community that shares a history and an aspiration, that provides an informing and corrective context; the circumstances being interpreted, while different from others, are also continuous with previous circumstances. Within these boundaries, there is no way absolutely to foreclose differences in evaluation, though there is a pressure to seek commonality. Theological interpretation of the significance of circumstances is fundamentally a historical, time-bound work; the kind of certitude that magisterial ecclesiastical authority sometimes seeks cannot exist. Not only the human condition but the multidimensional experience of the reality of God makes this so.

Thus the fifth criterion for the selection of symbols and concepts must be relatively loose and more complex than the other four. The appropriateness of religious symbols and of theological concepts for the interpretation of circumstances is subject to several tests. One is a theological norm of God's good will for creation, and the ways in which the symbols elucidate that (even symbols of judgment and wrath can do that). A second is their relevance to the events and circumstances. I indicated in chapter 1 that the very delineation of an "event" involves a prior evaluation of it. Theological concepts often are part of the theologian's disposition to describe its significance in particular ways. Yet this can be done with greater self-criticism. A third is an ethical test; the symbols and concepts ought to be tested by ethical concepts warranted by the symbols and the experiences of the religious community. The fourth is a social test; they are subject to critical scrutiny by others conscientiously engaged in the same activities. An element of individual subjective confirmation in experience is in the end unavoidable; while the interpreter can give reasons why he chooses the symbols that he does in relation to these four tests, there will always be a "confession" that they "make sense" to him.

The looseness of this proposal is regrettable, even to me. It surely appears too relative, too private, and insufficiently rational to many others. When I once described some of my work to a well-known moral philosopher, he was prompted to say, "It may be easier to find out what is right than to find out how Christians should go about deciding what is right." The point is cogent and the way it is made is forceful. It vitiates the enterprise, however, only if the religious dimensions of experience are not to be taken seriously. If a community experiences 'he reality of a power standing over against them, then its relations to that power are more inclusive than morality in a narrow sense encompasses. Its moral reflection takes place in the context of its religious experience. Thus the prior preoccupation is a religious one, a preoccupation with the relations of all things to God. Given this, in spite of its complexity and cumbersomeness, moral reflection has to be worked out in relation to religious symbols and theological concepts.

With such an elaborate approach, I would probably have interpreted the circumstances on Lexington Avenue to have the same moral significance as my friend, the moral virtuoso, saw in them. And the course of action he followed would probably also be one that would appear right to me. The point is not to say that in every instance the immediately pertinent (that is, to a required act) significance would be different because Christian symbols are used. There are occasions, however, on which a Christian *might* see a different significance, and a different attitude and course of action might follow.

Another illustration from my experience might make that clear. For several years I have periodically had intense discussions about human interventions into the "evolutionary process" with a philosophically sophisticated medical scientist. Our arguments are frequently unpersuasive to each other because of a difference in attitude toward many particular present and possible future interventions. He is more anxious than I am about the destructive possibilities and thus has favored more restrictive policies of control. On one occasion we agreed that what might make a crucial difference are my religious experiences and beliefs, and the symbols and concepts they provide me for interpreting the present and future significance of such interventions. Crucial was my affirmation of the goodness of the ultimate power, which coupled with other symbols in effect said we must be vigilant about interventions, but even out of particularly tragic irreversible mistakes can come possibilities for subsequent benefits. Without such beliefs and concepts he did not have the same attitude; there was less hopefulness in his. And without hopefulness, a more restrictive course of action seemed warranted to him. (It is also clear to me that my differences with theologians, such as Paul Ramsey, who favor more restrictive policies on these matters is a serious theological difference, and not only a moral one.)

Can ethics be Christian? In this chapter I have attempted to show how religious symbols and theological concepts are used to interpret the significance of circumstances and events in which persons are called upon to act. I have not argued that the *moral* significance disclosed in this process is unique. Indeed, with reference to biologists, it is clear that unlike my conversation partner referred to, many of them have a more hopeful attitude than he does on the basis of nonreligious beliefs. I have attempted to make a more modest claim, namely, that insofar as Christian symbols and concepts have a special claim on the religious community, they are used to disclose significance. That significance is preeminently religious and theological, but it is also in many instances moral. The religious significance impregnates the moral and may make a difference to the discernment of the moral. In this limited sense, then, the enterprise of ethical reflection may be distinctly Christian.

6 Religious Beliefs and the Determination of Conduct

In the previous four chapters I have sought to indicate some of the ways in which religious experience and religious beliefs have consequences for the morality of those who are engaged in religious life. In chapters 2 and 3 attention was focused on the formation of the moral agent. Religious experience and beliefs were shown to have a limited but nonetheless significant impact upon "the sort of person" one becomes. In chapter 4 the concern was for religious reasons for being moral, and an effort was made to indicate the personal and existential aspects of these reasons as well as the more rational aspects. Then I attempted in chapter 5 to demonstrate how religious symbols and theological concepts determine in part the evaluative description of what is going on; how this is correlated with attitudes toward events, and from it certain courses of action seem appropriate. In all of these aspects a restricted claim is plausible in support of characteristics distinctive not only to Christian morality but to the critical intellectual task of Christian ethics. The Christian theologian concerned with ethics necessarily must take these distinctively Christian aspects into account both in his work as the interpreter of the fundamental characteristics of Christian morality and in any normative or prescriptive work that he or she does.

In this chapter attention will be given to an issue to which I have pointed in previous chapters but have not isolated for intensive exploration. The focus is more on the *rational task* of relating religious *beliefs* to moral principles and moral values that are more directly action guiding in the rational determination of action than are dispositions, reasons for being moral, and the symbols that interpret the moral significance of events. We are here more concerned with beliefs than with believing, more concerned with rational discrimination and determination of conduct than with how actions "flow" from character or "follow" from an interpretation of an event. Attention will be given to what I judge to be a serious test for any claim to distinctiveness in Christian ethics. Are there ever occasions when the religious belief that justifies or perhaps determines moral action cannot be converted into a moral principle that excludes the particularities of that religious belief? Are there ever occasions, to restate the question, when a person might give a reason for acting that is so bound to his historical religious belief that nonreligious thinkers could not justify the action or principles that are universalizable? Are there moral actions that are mandatory for religious persons *only for "religious" or "Christian" reasons* and not for reasons on which all rational persons could presumably agree?

An inquiry guided by this intention would have been scorned by the man who knew what to do but was not concerned with why he did what he did on that summer night in New York. But the incident in which we participated can be used to illustrate the kinds of questions we are asking here. Before turning to them, however, we can see how the claims of the previous chapters might relate to a religious person's participation in that incident. To do so will help to distinguish more clearly what the special concern is in this chapter.

The course of action pursued on Lexington Avenue I would judge on the whole to be consistent with the characteristics of moral agents that religious experience of a Christian sort would foster. It is quite conceivable that those actions could have flowed "with ease" from deeply conscientious Christians. There was a readiness to seek the interests of another at the inconvenience (if not serious self-sacrificial costs) of my colleague's own self-interest. His disposition was to meet an immediate and apparent need of a "neighbor" whose personal history was unknown and with whom there were no previous ties of interest or affection. The attitude of will and mind was not retributive; rather, it was to avoid possibilities of greater harm to the soldier. But the intention to "do good" was not sentimental; if talking to the hotel management about the bartender's dishonesty was "retributive," there were reasons for it. Some institutional restraints on dishonesty were deemed to be required; the "law" had to be invoked to seek to insure subsequent honesty. These dispositions and the actions that followed could have been judged to be exemplary of the Christian moral life.

The moral conscientiousness of my colleague was equally exemplary of the Christian life. Reasons of mind and heart for being moral that I have developed would sustain his morality. Some of the same sorts of "senses" that I have shown to be correlated with the experience of the reality of God were present in him. There was a sense of direction that was in its moral aspects what a Christian should have; there was a sense of possibilities emerging in the interaction that a religious person would affirm to be grounded theologically; there was a sense of obligation to seek what is right and good. There was no proud self-righteousness, but there was a quiet confidence. His sensibilities, though not nurtured by religious life, were nonetheless what Christians often have, and surely ought to have.

Using Christian symbols, one would be likely to understand the moral significance of those circumstances in much the same way my companion did. The theological significance of the moral aspects would not be of any decisive importance in determining the moral significance in that particular instance. A concept of sin and moral evil would have yielded the same evaluation of the bartender's actions and character. A concept of God's willing man's good would have disclosed the same possibilities for beneficial responses there.

In this chapter we are concerned with another aspect of morality. Could I, as a theologian, have inferred from articulated Christian beliefs some action-guiding principles that ought to determine conduct in those circumstances? For example, to use a notion coined by Paul Ramsey, could a belief statement that God is love be "in-principled" in such a way that moral principles and rules of conduct would follow? How would one do that, if affirmative answers are correct?

Our harder test case would ask, with that bar-room incident in mind, would I have done anything that I judged to be morally right in that sequence of events for religious reasons that could not be converted into nonreligious moral reasons? That is, into reasons on which my secular partner and I could not agree upon as sufficient to justify and determine our conduct? (In that incident, the answer is negative, but there may be a special case in which it would be affirmative, as I shall indicate subsequently.)

Inferring Moral Principles from Religious Beliefs

That moral principles and moral values can somehow be derived from religious beliefs has been long and widely assumed, particularly in Protestant theological ethics. Just how they are derived and just what are the relations between religious beliefs and moral principles are matters open for discussion. Differences of opinion exist on these matters; both theological positions and philosophical assumptions are crucial in determining where particular persons or traditions take their stands on them.[1] Three questions are useful to ask in sorting out types of opinion. Does the ordering and articulation of beliefs about God see his relation to moral action as one that is mediated through an "ordering of creation" as a "natural law" or does it see his relation as more immediate—acting in events and human actions, commanding what is to be done in particular circumstances? Does Christian theology require that the Bible is the more immediate, and the exclusive source of knowledge of God, and thus the first reference for prescriptive Christian ethics, or is the relation of the Bible to ethics a more "remote" one? And, are the moral requirements for action derived by intuition from religious beliefs, or are they derived by a process of rational inference? For purposes of brevity, I wish to develop three types of opinion; answers to these questions are related to each other in different ways in each. Then I shall formulate my own opinion.

The first type enables us to see a pattern in an influential stream of Protestant thought in the middle period of our century. The relation of God to events is rather immediate; he is acting and commanding in them. The notion of God acting and commanding has its source in scripture, and it is to scripture that one turns to understand what God is doing or commanding. Since the moral response is to what God is now doing, or now commanding, it is necessary to have a sort of intuitive perception of that, rather than to draw more rational inferences from beliefs. I believe this constellation of judgments aids one to understand decisive issues in the theological ethics of Karl Barth, H. Richard Niebuhr, Paul Lehmann, and a major aspect of those of Emil Brunner.[2]

For all of these thinkers it is not unfair to say that the first question of practical moral reflection (moral *reasoning* may be too strong) is a theological question: "What is God doing (or saying)?" as both Niebuhr and Lehmann explicitly state.[3] The language used to elucidate the relation of God to the events and agents is drawn from personal life; as humans act in events, so God acts in events. It is not the language of a more remote relation; for example, God has created a moral order to which human institutions and events must conform. To learn what God is doing, one must look to the source where he revealed what he does, namely, to the Bible as a record of his activity in the lives of the Jewish community, Jesus, and the early Christian community. But since God is acting here and now, and since moral action is in response to God's present activity and commanding, that record cannot be a book of moral rules, or a collection of possible analogies to current events. Thus it is not a source for drawing rational inferences. As a consequence there is a highly intuitive aspect to determining what human agents ought to do; indeed at least for Barth agents are to be determined (in their freedom) by God's command.

This type of opinion lays the groundwork for the claim of great distinctiveness, if not uniqueness for Christian ethics. That the first practical question is a theological one, and that the best insight into its answer is to be found in the Christian scriptures is sufficient to make the point. What human agents do is right (not only religiously but also morally) insofar as it conforms with God's activity, endorses what he is doing, or is obedient to his command. The distinctiveness is qualified, however, by the high degree of assurance that God does and commands what is morally right for, or morally beneficial to, the human community. Lehmann, for example, states as his central theme that God is engaged in "humanizing activity," that he is acting "to make and keep human life human." Perception of what God is doing or commanding is perception of what is morally right and good in this type. Yet it is morally right and good in this type because *God* is doing or commanding it; hence it is to knowledge of God's activity and commands that agents must first turn.[4]

Other matters can be correlated with what I have stated as salient aspects of this type, such as (in some authors) a strong sense of divine determinism, but for our purposes the implications for the determination of conduct are most significant. By now they are clear. It is not so much that action-guiding moral principles and values are "derived from" beliefs, as it is that in believing and knowing God to be present, agents are to be receptive to his actions and commands. The rational processes are in various measures short-circuited in this type. That I will not defend this type will become clear.

The second type enables us to see a pattern that has dominated Catholic theological ethics since the Middle Ages and that is present in some aspects of the Protestant tradition. The relation of God to events is more "remote" than it is in the first type; he created the world with a *telos*, an end, that inheres in nature, or he created the world in an "order of creation" that is in some sense present in human institutions and their relations to each other. Thus to gain insight into what God's will is, or what is morally right and good, one does not necessarily turn to scripture. Scripture gives insight into the "fact" that the world was created by God, but the creation itself is a source of moral values and principles. Indeed, the morality that scripture teaches is, on the whole, a confirmation of the morality that inheres in the creation. To determine what human action should be, then, agents rationally reflect upon the natural law or on the orders of creation. Since all men have those capacities (by nature, created by God) there is a theological authorization for "natural morality." Yet, there must be some way to account for the very demanding statements of Jesus, and for the occasions in scripture on which God seems to have commanded irrational and immoral acts; how these are accounted for is different in various theologies. This constellation of judgments aids our understanding not only of Catholic ethics but also of aspects of the ethics of Calvin and Luther.[5]

In these traditions it is fair to claim that two sources of moral knowledge have great, if not equal, authority: the ordering of creation and scripture. In the Catholic tradition the practice of reflection on nature, and on the natural law, has been most important. Frequently biblical texts have been used to give additional "proof" to the conclusions of rational reflection. Where scriptural accounts contradict these conclusions, "secret" commands of God have been invoked.[6] But apart from these few "exceptions," in principle all rational persons can agree on what is morally right and good. The "hard" commands of Jesus become "evangelical counsels," not moral principles, and are applicable only to those who have special vocations to obey them. They are not requirements made of all Christians, not to mention all human beings.

Two aspects of Luther's ethics can be distinguished in a way that has some formal similarities to the Catholic tradition. The Christian has no privileged position from which to know what ought to be done in ordering social, economic, and political life. While he "knows" that the requirements for the ordering of society, and of his role or office in society, are ways in which God is ruling through the political use of his law, through the strange works of his love, this, on the whole, makes no significant difference in comparison with the non-Christian in what he is required to do, or in how he discerns what he ought to do. It is through the use of reason that the Christian, like the Turk, learns what justice is and requires in particular circumstances. His acts are intentionally obedient to God, but the visable "shape" of his obedient action in these arenas of life cannot be distinguished from that of others. Thus all reasonable persons ought to be able to agree on what is morally required by reflecting on the orders of creation. There is another aspect to the moral actions of Christians, however. They have a new inner disposition, and in grateful response to God's redeeming love for them, they meet, in love, the neighbor's deepest need. It is not that they owe allegiance to "evangelical counsels," but that they are moved in and by love toward others. In this regard an intuitive element is implicit; they need no steps of practical moral reasoning to determine the neighbor's need, though examples (such as how the Christian prince will act) and exhortations are in order.[7] The new disposition might make some difference in what the Christian does in his "office," thus the qualification, "on the whole," above. But the determination of conduct in social roles and institutions is arrived at by the use of reason. These roles and institutions are "masks of God"; one senses in Luther that God's presence through them has a greater immediacy than God's presence through the natural law the Catholic tradition. It is the voice of God that is heard through the requirements of roles and institutions. For religious and theological reasons Luther rejects the highly developed account of "nature" that Thomas has; and thus the reasoning does not have the precision and discriminations that it has in the Catholic tradition. Nonetheless, the "orders" have a measure of autonomy as a source of moral principles.

Calvin's understanding of the relation of natural law and scripture as two sources is different from these two, and more complex. He can be intensely biblical (indeed, N. H. G. Robinson calls him fundamentalistic) and have a high confidence in natural law at the same time.[8] The decalogue is in its essence a statement of the natural law, and the teachings of Jesus clarify its obscurities and blemishes. This identification of the basic biblical moral teachings with the natural law, it seems to me, permits Calvin to do two things in a distinctive way. He can elucidate what he sees to be implications of biblical moral teachings with a confidence that what he writes is of moral authority for all men, and he does not have to make the same division between "evangelical counsels" and ethics that the dominant Catholic tradition has done.[9] There are special requirements of the Christian life, such as "cross-bearing" in imitation of Christ, but these are for all Christians and not just those with a special "religious" vocation.

The coherence of elements in the delineation of this second type, however, is more pertinent to my present intention than is the interpretation of writings in the light of it. The basic point is that something designated "nature," whether it assumes an Aristotelian meaning or not, or something called "orders of creation," is the basis on which rational reflection determines principles and rules of moral conduct. God is the creator of this nature, or these orders; but agents do not need to know that or believe that to determine what is morally right. And, on the whole, the historically positive or particular book, the Bible, in its basic moral teachings is a "revealed" source of what persons, in principle, have the natural capacities to know. There is a basis for rational inferences to be drawn from "nature," though in practice it was not always used. To know what God wills, persons need to know what is required by reason, or by nature.

This type of position claims no uniqueness for "Christian ethics" insofar as that term refers to the prescriptive task necessary to determine what conduct ought to be in ordinary human relations. Whether there is distinctiveness depends upon whether other considerations are permitted within the bounds of the term ethics. That each of the authors referred to claims something distinctive for Christian behavior can be sustained. Though I have not developed this, it is fair to say that all would claim that in the faith and life of the Christian community there are "means of grace" that have consequences for motives (both in terms of reasons for acting and in terms of the moving of human capacities to act). The Catholic tradition has claimed particular obligations for those who take religious vows, and has especially honored many who have "turned the other cheek" or "gone the second mile," but in a strict sense there are no *moral* obligations to do these things. The Protestant writers exhort or require particularly "Christian" behavior on the part of those who have faith; they are to follow Christ in meeting the needs of others as he has met their needs, that is, in "love" and in self-sacrifice. In a sense it is fair to say, then, that there is a special ethics for Christians in addition to theologically grounded ethics that apply to all. These obligations are not merely "religious" obligations; they are also moral obligations within a "way of life" that Christians have been called to for more than moral reasons.[10] On these grounds the "Christian" cannot be converted into "the

natural" or "the human" without remainder, though "the natural" and "the human" are aspects of "Christian ethics," on the
theological grounds of the doctrine of creation.

A third type enables us to elucidate some of the pattern of a
great deal of American Protestant ethics. The relation of God to
events is not discussed; it certainly is not as immediate as it is in
the first type. But moral teachings, for some reasons, are to be
derived from the theological and ethical teachings of the scriptures. Since the mode of "derivation" does not permit a "literal"
application to contemporary events, a process of drawing inferences from scripture to formulate moral principles and values is
necessary, as is a process for "applying" them to moral action.
Whether the principles and their application cohere or do not
cohere with universalizable principles established by "natural"
reason is not a serious concern. The point is that "Christian
ethics" is assumed to be possible, and is a matter of deep
practical importance for the Christian churches.

As an ideal construct, this type enables us to see a pattern that
in important respects is present in such otherwise diverse authors
as Walter Rauschenbusch, Reinhold Niebuhr, John C. Bennett,
and Paul Ramsey. None of them develops very fully the most
technically theological dimensions of ethics, that is, the doctrine
of God; all of them assume a significant authority of scripture,
particularly the New Testament; each of them has a way of
inferring moral principles and values from the New Testament
via social ideals judged to be implicit in the idea of the Kingdom
of God, the dialectical relations of agape and justice, middle
axioms, or "in-principled" love.

Some claim for a revelation of God's will is implicit in all
authors to whose work this type is applicable. In no instance is it
claimed that the significance of that revelation is private, that is,
for Christians only. There is a universal significance to it. In the
case of Reinhold Niebuhr, for example, what is disclosed in the
biblical accounts is confirmed in experience—man's basic anxiety
in his freedom, his seeking to overcome it through pride and
sensuality, and so forth. Also Niebuhr affirms that "love is the
law of life."[11] What is central to the Christian story is thus of
universal significance. Rauschenbusch makes a claim that is

similar in its formal aspects. The will of God, a central New Testament symbol, "is identical with the good of mankind."[12] For this social gospel reformer and scholar the terms "Kingdom of God" and "the good of mankind" become convertible. As a result of this, what is inferred from the biblical symbol is of universal significance; also what one perceives on other grounds to be "the good of mankind" can be used to elucidate the symbol of the Kingdom. Paul Ramsey construes his practical ethics to be executed by formulating moral principles and rules of conduct that are implicit in the Christian notion of love. The universal significance of the Christian notion of love is backed by distinctively Christian affirmations, such as "Jesus Christ is Lord."[13] The inferences drawn from love on a rational basis are in principle applicable to all over which Jesus is Lord, that is, to all persons.

The type is characterized by using biblical teachings of Jesus or the prophets, or biblical events such as the crucifixion, as a basis for more precise determination of action-guiding moral ideals or moral principles. Rauschenbusch seems to infer from biblical teaching the social moral ideals that human action ought to realize, for example, a democratized society in economic as well as social and political terms. This ideal in turn warrants specific proposals, such as national ownership of natural resources. John C. Bennett develops "middle axioms" that are more precise in their references than the seemingly vague general principle of love, but are not so precise as to determine action in all particular circumstances. Ramsey has sought to make a case for "unexceptionable rules" of conduct.[14] The process of moving to action-guiding principles and rules is much more rational than is the intuitive process of discerning what God is doing or commanding in the first type. In distinction from the use of natural law and orders of creation in the second type, those whose work I have used to illustrate this type *tend* to eschew the metaphysical dimensions of such proposals and thus to use the Bible in a more immediate way.

This type seems to involve the claim for a unique Christian revelation that is morally very important (it is not only a revelation of a "saving" reality). Thus even social ethics is conducted with reference to the specific Christian body of literature. To some extent this is done for practical reasons; part of the audience to whom the writings are addressed is the Christian community. There is a stronger reason for this, however, in the judgment that what is particularly made known in the biblical teachings is "the law of life." To those who are not persuaded of this, the third type looks highly particularistic in its Christian basis; to those who are persuaded, the particularistic historical basis is not of private significance, though a special claim exists on those who are Christians. In the authors I have cited there is a way to move from the heedless love of the Christian teachings to inferences that in the eyes of some Christian critics compromise the radical character of what is uniquely Christian.[15] Both theological and ethical arguments are made to justify these moves; whatever they are they support a claim that the Christian ethic is one of cultural and social responsibility in relation to events and circumstances, and not one that calls for an exemplary community demonstrating a "higher way" in a sinful world. The form of that responsibility is not only, or even principally, one of protest, but also one of participation in established institutions of power in society. What is to the critic mistaken compromise is to the defender of this type an obligation to relate specifically Christian norms and values to contemporary events.

I would defend a position that emphasizes the necessity of rationally drawing moral inferences from religious beliefs to develop moral values and principles for the guidance of action. The context in which that is done, however, is a complex one and includes aspects of all three of the ideal-types I have constructed.[16]

Like the first type, I would affirm that the experience of the reality of God is one of the presence of a dynamic (a power) that is purposive. The ultimate one to whom men are responding and to whom they are accountable is God, this power. Christian morality has a definite theological dimension; Christian "prescriptive" ethics therefore necessarily must be *theo*logical ethics. Unlike the first type, however, I would not state the first practical question to be, "What is God doing?" or "What is God commanding?" Rather, the primary question (though not necessarily chronologically the first) is, "What is God enabling and requiring me (or us) to be and to do?" There are two reasons for the alteration. First, to be able to say "what God is doing" with specificity and certitude is not a human possibility. At issue may be whether persons of profound faith can see what he is doing or hear what he is commanding, while persons of "weaker" faith cannot. There is, however, no verifiable way to test the most faithful person's clarity and subjective certitude. Given the assumptions that any experience of God is mediated and not direct, all perceptions of his presence are opaque. Although for purposes of theological clarity it would be desirable to distinguish precisely between what God is doing and what persons are doing, my view of the experience of God does not make that possible.

The second reason for the alteration is that what follows from perceiving God's action, namely, a somewhat passive conformity of human action to it, violates human agency. It too readily authorizes a view of divine determinism that renders the capacities of humans to determine their responses and the exercises of power by their own intentions a mere shadow. My reformulation of the primary question, "What is God enabling and requiring me (us) to be and to do?" is grounded in an affirmation of greater human autonomy, that is, in a view of persons and communities as agents.

These two reasons do not, however, render useless the human effort to discern what God is requiring and enabling. Statements about the purposes of the ultimate power have been made on the basis of long experience in the religious communites. The articulation of these experiences provides the *beliefs* that the Christian community uses. It seeks to infer from these beliefs moral values and principles that shed some light on what God is enabling and requiring in current events and circumstances. The rational process of drawing inferences occurs in the lived experience of the community. The principles and values inferred illuminate what God *might* be requiring and enabling us to do in our circumstances. There are occasions when all doubt about the rightness of specific action is erased, but even in these the certitude that human action is determined by God's command is not possible. On many occasions where conflicts of moral values exist in relation to particular circumstances doubt remains, but action must be taken. The moral principles and values inferred from beliefs guide human actions but do not provide absolute certitude that these actions are perfectly in accord with God's purposes.

Similar to the second type I would affirm that inferences drawn from wide ranges of human experience give us insight into the basic moral values and principles, or the fundamental "moral requisites," for human life. Unlike this type, however, on epistemological grounds, I am not prepared to affirm that these inferences give knowledge (in the strongest sense) of the moral order and end of creation. The difference between classic natural law theory and what I propose is important; generalizations about the moral values and principles which provide the conditions *sine qua non* for human personal and social life can be made. Classic natural law theory is based on the epistemological asumption that there is a correspondence between the order of the human mind and the order of being, whereas I would propose a "weaker" view. An intelligible account of experience that issues in "almost universal" and "almost absolute" principles and values can be given, but the conditions of knowledge do not exist on which universality and absoluteness can be claimed without qualification. Necessary moral conditions for human life to be fulfilled in any satisfactory sense can be stated, but these statements are inferences from experience and not knowledge of being.

The theological warrant for drawing such inferences is the presence of the ultimate and purposive power in events and in experience. To perceive these necessary conditions is to perceive some signals about what God is requiring humans to be and to do. Thus from a theological point of view the rational process of drawing moral inferences from human experience and stating these in terms of "almost absolute" values and principles is proper. Further and more precise action-guiding values and principles applicable to diverse circumstances, events, and agents are also warranted; these also illumine or guide the human search to discern what God is enabling and requiring me (us) to be and to do. Intuitive (in a strong sense) perceptions, for example, of what it means to be human are open to too little self-criticism if this more self-critical process is omitted. To rely on immediate sensitivity to what God in his freedom is doing in the world to make and keep human life human, as Paul Lehmann suggests, is theologically and philosophically defensible only on grounds that I find unsupportable.[17]

The possibility of inferring general values and principles from experience assumes that the continuities in human experience are greater than are the discontinuities. To state that distributive justice is a necessary condition for a modicum of harmony in human societies, for example, is to make a claim based on not just the experience of one generation, or of one nation. The import of this observation is met on two margins. First, the radical occasionalism of moral responses that is found frequently in the first type is wrong. While specific occasions calling for human action are distinctive, and in the precise combination of elements even unique, the continuities and general characteristics of occasions are sufficient to warrant the exercise of analogical thinking from one event to another, and inference drawing from the more general values and principles to the particular. To view life as "history" and not as "immutable nature" does not entail the absolute uniqueness of occasions that in turn require a unique perception of what is uniquely right, or a private and unique command of God.

Second, on the theological margin, some theological ethical occasionalists are deeply concerned to preserve the freedom of God, though they also affirm a divine decision by God to limit his freedom to the revelation of his graciousness in Christ, or apparently to do what makes and keeps human life human. Whether God freely chose to have the purpose for human well-being that I affirm he has, is not a matter of great importance to our intentions here. To assume the reliability of inferences of almost absolute values and principles from a great range of human experience, and to do so with a *theo*logical point of reference, is to claim that the ultimate power is, in effect, limited to the purposes that are perceived to inhere in creation, and by the conditions necessary to fulfill to some extent these purposes. If one chose with Lehmann to say that God does what makes and keeps human life human, and if "human" is a highly value-laden term in this phrase, as surely it is, then the limitation of God's intention to the "normatively human" justifies and demands reflection on what the valued or normative qualities of humanity are. The limitation of God establishes the basis for rational inferences from the general qualities by which his intentions are presumably limited.

Radical occasionalism in theological ethics is based on the premise that God's "freedom," while bound by his choice, still might erupt in actions that could not be anticipated by the exercise of human rational capacities. I have Karl Barth's theological ethics particularly in mind here. Even the most unanticipated action of God would be a gracious action, not because its moral rightness was not humanly discerned but in principle could be, but because it would be his gracious act (by choice that is the only sort he does). In accord with the weight I have given to the autonomy of human agents, on those few occasions when a human action is one that could not be anticipated by knowing what values and principles the agent adhered to, the uniqueness of any act would be premised not on a free and unique command of God but on a unique perception by the agent that the act was required of him. As a religious person he believes it is what God requires him to do, and he might give reasons for this, at least after the fact. But the accountability for the perception is his; he cannot defer it to God.

The affinity of my views with at least one aspect of the third type is now clear, namely, that which rationally draws moral inferences from religious beliefs. My views differ from the third type in two important ways. First, the intention of the rational process of drawing inferences from beliefs and applying them to circumstances of action is to discern what the dynamic of God's presence and purposes are. There is less "distance" between God and the immediately present circumstances and agents than is characteristic of the third type. Second, I would be clearer than the third type is about the grounds for using a wide range of human experience as a source for the derivation of moral norms and values, in addition to scripture.

Scripture is used in various ways in all three types. To clarify my own position it is necessary to indicate carefully how scripture is used in it, and particularly the distinctively Christian accents or aspects of the scriptures. By exploring this we will come to a major question, namely, are there "Christian" principles and values that have a particular obligatory character for members of the Christian community?

In other parts of the book some points have been made that are important to recall here. First, I have suggested that scripture gives us accounts of the interpretation of events and articulated beliefs that arise out of the people's experience of God's presence and power. Second, what gives the scriptures some authority for us is neither a fundamentalistic view nor the view that an ecclesiastical decision was made to close the canon, but rather that the perceptions of the meaning of God's presence recorded there are to some extent confirmed in our current experience in the Christian and wider community. That something circular is involved in this must be frankly admitted; since the symbols and beliefs of scripture nourish and inform the contemporary experience, there is a predisposition to the confirmation of its meanings. Precisely because we are exposed to and seriously use other symbols, concepts, and beliefs, as well as those of scripture, however, there is a testing of the adequacy of its terms. The present community's experiences are sufficiently continuous with and similar to those of the biblical people to give scripture authority; they are sufficiently discontinuous and different to require other "authorities" as well. We have also noted the plurality of symbols and concepts in scripture, and the need for a governing principle to give some order to the variety.

The central symbol for Christians historically has been Jesus Christ, and if a contemporary community is to be denominated "Christian" it makes sense to assume that such primacy and centrality be acknowledged. The Christian experience of the reality of God is informed by the accounts of Christ that were recorded in the early church. There is also a confirmation in the experience of Christians that through Christ, as depicted in these accounts, the perception of God's intentions for humans and the rest of creation has a particular compelling clarity. This compelling clarity gives Christ a unique authority for Christians. Indeed, this compelling clarity has been the necessary condition for all the Christological doctrines of the scriptures and subsequent theologies. In effect these doctrines have been explanations of how this could be. On the premise that God was experienced through Jesus speculative inferences have been drawn to show the necessary and sufficient conditions for this experience. Among those aspects of God's intentionality that have been perceived through Jesus are his moral purposes, his intention toward the well-being of persons and community.

On these grounds, then, Jesus Christ, and the documents through which his significance is communicated, take on a distinctive authority for ethics as well as for theology in the Christian community. To make the case boldly, if the experience of reality of God, informed by scripture and particularly by Jesus, is not one of compelling clarity, the task of developing any distinctively Christian ethics would at best be a hypothetical exercise. For those for whom there is a compelling clarity to the experience of God through the scriptures and Jesus, it is worthwhile to infer rationally the principles and values that would direct a "way of life" that is grounded in Jesus and the scriptures.[18] Those for whom Jesus has this authority ought to be guided by certain moral principles and moral values in their actions. Part of the task of the theologian is to stipulate what principles and values can be reasonably inferred from the biblical accounts of Jesus and his significance.

He does not begin *de novo*, however, for the biblical accounts themselves have done this in different forms of rhetoric. Some, like moral teachings attributed to Jesus himself, are immediately and directly to the point of the theologian's ethical task. Others, like certain parables, require more complex interpretation to understand and perhaps can provide analogies that are action guiding. Narratives of Jesus's deeds are at least illustrations of what forms of action cohere with an experience of the ultimate power. Christians ought to do things similar to what Jesus did. Statements of beatitudes are not only counsels of prudence—if you wish to see the Kingdom of God you ought to be poor in spirit—but also a basis for inferring the sorts of values that persons faithful to Jesus ought to have. The primacy, but not exclusivity, of love—as disposition, as referring to a quality of interrelations, as something commanded—creates an "accented note" in the score of Christian "prescriptive" ethics. An "inprincipling" of love is warranted for Christian ethics to develop action-guiding principles. In effect, actions that are faithful to the perceptions of the reality of God through Jesus should be guided by principles and values that are coherent with the significance of Christ. The New Testament writings in various ways already do that.

The formal process of Christian "prescriptive" ethics is a continuation of this. The community of Christians is the primary audience for such work. The Christian theologian's ethical task is engaged in for the sake of the community that shares a set of common experiences and beliefs. Calvin was correct in making "the third use of the law" the principal one; the Christian community needs some instruction and guidance to determine the sorts of actions that are the morally proper expressions of its experience of God.

The Christian community is not, however, the exclusive audience. Since the intention of the divine power for human well-being is universal in its scope, the historically particular medium through which that power is clarified for Christians also has universal significance. The theologian engaged in the task of "prescriptive" ethics formulates principles and values that can guide the actions of persons who do not belong to the Christian community. They will be persuasive to others, however, on the basis of supporting reasons different from those that Christians might respond to. In effect, the theologian moves from the particular Christian belief to a statement of their moral import in a more universal language. These statements will be persuasive to nonreligious persons only by the cogency of the argument that is made to show that the "historical particularity" sheds light on principles and values that other serious moral persons also perceive and also ought to adhere to. Indeed, since the Christian theologian shares in the general moral experiences of secular people, and since one facet of his work that is theologically warranted is the inferring of principles and values from common experience, he or she need not in every practical circumstance make a particular theological case for what is formulated. The theologian ought, however, to be able to make a Christian theological case if challenged to do so. To make the point in a pithy way, Christian ethics (in terms not only of action-guiding principles and values, but also in terms of justifications for these) can in large measure be converted into "natural" or "rational" ethics. "In large measure" is an important qualification, for I aspire to demonstrate that they cannot be converted without remainder.

What is the remainder? The answer is not simple. In the concluding chapter a more comprehensive effort is made to address head on (relying on the previous chapters) the question, "Can ethics be Christian?" Here we shall note that the distinctive media through which Christians experience reality of God with compelling clarity are not judged to be accidental to that experience. Nor would most contemporary theologians, including me, judge that these media are *necessary* to experience the reality of God, that is, that the reality of the ultimate power standing over against the world can be known only through Jesus and the Christian scriptures. That Christians do perceive that power and its purposes with compelling clarity through these media, however, warrants taking the media in an especially serious, that is, authoritative way. Thus there are some special obligations for Christians. An example, and in my judgment the best one, is the obligation of the imperative, "Let no one seek his own good, but the good of his neighbor." In this form, the statement is found in 1 Corinthians 10:24; the apostle Paul in his letter to the Philippian Christians states a less rigorous obligation, "Let each of you look not only to his own interests, but also to the interests of others" (Phil. 4:2). Similar to this in their special rigor are the commands of Jesus to "go the second mile," to give not only one's cloak but one's coat also, and "to love one's enemies." In their morally rigorous forms, each of these diminishes the centrality that "rational self-interest" often has in other forms of ethics. Indeed, these statements do not counsel that by seeking the interests of others, one's own "true" or "real" interests are fulfilled, though such justifications for them are often given.

These rigorous obligations are reasonably inferred from, and perhaps even "entailed" by (morally, not necessarily logically in a strict sense) the compelling clarity of God's reality as a power of love, indeed, a love that sacrifices its own "immediate interests"

for the sake of others. More concisely, the centrality of the crucifixion in the Christian experience of God's reality requires that
those who have this belief also have obligations that are especially
binding on them. What Christians are obligated to do might well
be done by others on the basis of *moral ideals* that require more
than obligations defensible on the grounds of rational self-interest
can sustain. I am arguing, however, that Christians have an *obligation* to be governed by such action-guiding principles. The thrust
of these principles and their concurrent obligations is not exclusively toward the actions of individuals in relation to other individuals, though in many forms of popular Christianity this is the case.
They have implications for social and political life as well. In the
realm of social life "philanthropy" is not their only form; the
Christian community and its members have obligations in many
circumstances to be engaged in costly actions of resistance to
unjust and repressive social institutions, to costly participation in
struggles to achieve greater distributive justice in society.[19]

   If the cross informs experience of something essential about
the intentionality of the ultimate power, are not all persons
obligated to be guided by these rigorous principles? If the
religious dimensions of experience were convertible into a perception of ultimate reality as it is in and of itself, the answer would be
affirmative. On the premise that Christians have an epistemological privilege that enables them to articulate the principles of
ultimate reality, of the being of God with such objectivity that all
persons should be persuaded on rational grounds, it could be
argued that the answer is affirmative. Precisely this premise is not
consistent with the understanding of the religious dimensions of
experience developed in this book. The "experiential confirmation" is sufficiently relative to particular communities and persons not to warrant such a universal claim. The confirmation is
sufficiently strong, however, to warrant the claim that for those
who share it there are particular and distinctive obligations.

   Whether these obligations are deemed "moral" or "religious,"
whether the principles are deemed "ethical" or "religious," both
depend upon prior judgments about the use of the concepts
"moral" and "ethical." If a principle is ethical, per definition, only
if it is obligatory upon all persons, or if it can be justified only on

grounds on which all rational persons could agree, we have left "ethics" for "religion." If, however, distinctive obligations follow from a "way of life" to which one is committed, then these are moral obligations to moral principles that follow from a distinctively Christian experience and way of life. The choice of that way of life is not purely arbitrary, that is, totally irrational. One can give reasons for believing what Christians believe, though they will not be fully persuasive to those for whom these beliefs are not confirmed experientially. I am increasingly persuaded that no other definable "ways of life" including the most "rationally defensible" ones, and those that require the greatest rational disinterestedness to pursue, are exempt from some sort of confirmation in the experience of adherents.

A more precise test case is now in order. Is it conceivable that members of the Christian community would act under any circumstances in a way that could not be justified by principles on which presumably all rational persons could agree? Is it conceivable that a "moral" act by a Christian can be justified by only a "religious" reason, to refer to the distinction noted in the previous paragraph? I believe that such occasions would be extremely rare, and for reasons that are theological in character. Since God's purposes are believed to be for the well-being of man and creation, on most occasions the reasons that justify any moral act would justify the moral acts of Christians. Rare as they might be, an example will indicate such an occasion to be not only historically possible (there are Christians like those in the example) but reasonably so.

The example is that of highly confessional Christian nonviolence in resistance to evil. The "highly confessional" provides the clue to the possibility. Nonviolence in resistance to evil can be justified on a number of grounds. Respect for physical life is one; obedience to the commandment "Thou shalt not kill" is another. Appeals can be made to potential consequences; "he who lives by the sword shall perish by the sword"; violence begets violence, and much of value to all concerned is destroyed. Or, if all persons acted according to moral rules that prohibit violence we would have a more peaceful world. Highly confessional Christian pacifists may, or may not, concur in these reasons; what is decisive to them is that to act violently in resistance to evil is inconsistent with their commitment and loyalty to Jesus Christ, and to the Christian "way of life." It is a violation of the way of the cross. What makes violent action wrong for them is precisely this, or what makes it decisively wrong for them is this violation. For those who do not have this commitment, or for those who derive their moral principles from other bases, it may not be morally wrong. With this commitment and its attendant obligations it is wrong.

Is such a principle of nonviolence a moral principle? If, by definition, no such "private" reasons as a religious commitment can be used to support a *moral* principle, it is not. Rather it is a religious principle. If "moral" is used in a less restrictive sense, it is. It is a moral principle because actions governed by it have moral, or at least human value consequences for others. Not all such consequences in some circumstances would be judged praiseworthy by many persons, for example, deaths of others that could have been prevented by a violent act on the part of such a religious person. It is a moral principle in the sense that it determines the "conscience" of the believer; his moral integrity would be violated by violating the principle. Within a confessional Christian way of life that accents pacifism, it is morally wrong to act violently. If consequences judged to be evil occur as a result, from another point of view someone could charge that that way of life is immoral. But from within, the response, unpersuasive as it would be to those unsympathetic to it, would be that the reasons for adhering to that way of life are not merely moral ones; there is a confirmation in experience that persons are called to be obedient to that way of life.

The discussion of this chapter can be located on a larger map of theological ethics. Two extreme types of positions are possible. One is that Christian principles of action are always defensible on rational moral grounds; the "Christian" and the "rational moral" are convertible. The other is that to be Christian is to follow a certain moral way of life decisively, primarily or even exclusively because of a special calling to be the followers of Jesus. Other reasons for adhering to certain principles and values are secondary at best, and perhaps irrelevant. I have attempted to make a case that fits neither extreme. Nor does it divide the moral life of Christians between natural ethics and counsels of perfection, between life in the orders of Creation with one morality applicable to it, and life in faith with a new motive for life in the orders. The crucial point is that the media through which God's universal purposes for men and creation are experienced with compelling clarity take on a special authority for those who share that experience. That authority does not lead to a whole unique set of moral values and principles for Christians, but there are certain principles and values that can be rationally inferred from the historically particular media that might direct action in a distinctive way.

The whole discussion would be trivial to my colleague at the bar. It is, after all, the sort of nonsense that intellectuals are overpaid to play with. As I noted, nothing done by him individually or by us together in that barroom incident would have been guided by Christian principles and values that could not be justified on other grounds. The Christian in such circumstances, however, has a special obligation to act, he is to seek not his own interests (convenience in that time and place) but the interests of others (the needs of the soldier). That principle can be rationally inferred from Christian beliefs about God's purposes, from the symbol of the cross, though nothing like the cost of life was required there. In more critical circumstances, however, obedience to that principle might well be "obedience unto death." Such obedience is not easily justified on the basis of rational self-interest, or even on a proper balance of self-regard and other-regard.

7 Can Ethics Be Christian? Some Conclusions

Can ethics be Christian? The answer is negative if certain restrictive concepts of "ethics" are used. If the concept stipulates that any reflection on morality that finds justification or warrants for moral values and principles which are themselves grounded in "private," "historically particularistic," or "nonrational" assumptions is not ethical reflection, then in principle ethics cannot be Christian. If a pattern of thought, in order to be ethics, must in each order of moral discourse be exclusively rational, and if Christianity (or any other religion) is classed as irrational or nonrational, and if particular religious warrants are appealed to in any order of moral discourse, Christian moral thought is not ethics. For example, if the principle "you shall love your neighbor as yourself" is justified on the basis that it is in the Torah and in the Christian scriptures, or that it is a revelation from God, or that it is an action-guiding principle that is inferred from the theological assertion that God is love, then on the basis of the restrictive concept the process is not in the domain of ethics. If, however, that principle were justified on the grounds that it is a universalizable principle, and therefore one on which presumably all rational persons can agree, the process would be in the realm of ethics. Indeed, the biblical language might be interpreted to mean that one ought to respect each person as an end in himself, or in some similar way, in order to cleanse it of its particular historical religious overtones.

Even with a restrictive concept in mind, however, the matter is more complex than the previous paragraph has indicated. A principle like the love commandment, and most moral principles and values that guide the actions of Christians, can be generalized, if not applied universally; they can be defended on grounds that do not in the first instance make particular religious or theological appeals. Thus, it might be argued that the morality of the Christian community, or any other religious community, is in the domain of "ethics" insofar as it is "rationally" defensible. It could be excluded from ethics in any order of moral discourse in which the justifying principle was "religious." For example, if a Christian community claimed to obey the love commandment *only* because it was an obligation entailed by its fidelity to Jesus, the commandment would not be "ethical." If the community claimed, in the fashion of many Catholic and Protestant theologians, that the commandment is part of the "natural law" and thus can be known by all reasonable persons, it would be ethical. Insofar as an additional order of discourse was invoked, namely, the more ultimate justification for the natural law, and if Christians then justified adherence to natural law on the basis that it is a gift of God's graciousness in creation, then they would have left the arena of ethics. What was an ethical justification in one order of discourse is further justified in this instance by a nonethical, or theological warrant. If the theological appeal in this order is judged to be incidental or accidental, rather than intrinsic or necessary, to the morality of Christians, it can be asserted that the morality of the Christian community is in the domain of ethics but that Christians are "ethical" for a different general reason than secular rational persons are.

Can ethics be Christian? The answer is affirmative in a more forceful way than conclusions following from these chapters can be stated, on the basis of two different points of view. They are, first, that ethics must be Christian and *is* Christian in a universally applicable sense because it is in Christ that all things are created, and he is the Lord of all things. The second is that the ethics *of Christians* is and must be exclusively Christian because the community is called to absolute obedience to Jesus as Lord; all of the moral actions of the community must be determined by his lordship.

From the first point of view, Christian ethics and universal human ethics are convertible terms. What is ethically justifiable to do (in a purely rational sense) is the Christian thing to do, and vice versa. This is given theological legitimacy by the doctrine of the Trinity in which Christ, the second person, is the one in and through whom all things are created. From this point of view, in principle there is no distinctive Christian morality, but all morality that is rationally justifiable is Christian. The historical particularity of the source of the life of the church has no particular ethical significance, though its theological significance is tremendous, for Jesus is the revelation of God. Christians have special obligations perhaps, for example, to follow Jesus in lives of self-sacrificial service, but these are not ethical obligations. They are particular religious obligations. Christians have distinctive ideals, but these cannot be called, in a strict sense, moral ideas, for they are not rationally justifiable. If one chooses to call these obligations and ideals "moral," necessarily one has a double ethics, a minimalistic one that is Christian in a grand theological sense, and a more demanding one that is Christian in a special historical sense. With modifications, this point of view can be found in St. Thomas, Luther, and Calvin.[1]

From the second point of view that comes to a strong affirmative answer, not only can ethics be Christian, but the ethics of Christians *must be* Christian. The pattern for this has two distinctive points of orientation. One is that the Christian community has a particular vocation to follow Jesus and the way of life that he exemplified and taught; it is obligated to be fully obedient to his lordship, to be a distinctive people with a distinctive way of life. The second is that while Christ is confessed to be the savior of the world, the sorts of philosophical speculations that give grounds for the convertibility of the Christian and the rational are eschewed. The Christian community has its significant grounding in a historical event, and its history and conduct are to be determined by that historical revelation. This point of view does not imply that every moral act of Christians is distinctively different from the acts of other persons. The honesty of Christians, for example, in their personal or business relations has no visible difference from the honesty of other persons.

Indeed, the immediate moral intention of their actions (the intention to be honest) is not distinctive; they would also justify honesty on rational ethical grounds. What is characteristic, however, is that the final justification for honesty would be its consistency with a Christian way of life; a people could not be obedient to the lordship of Jesus and be dishonest. Very important for understanding this point of view is this: Jesus, who is Lord, is known through the gospel accounts of his life and teachings; on the basis of these accounts there are distinctive obligations for his followers and these are of equal authority to the more ordinary moral obligations that also follow from his lordship. "Christian" ethics then is highly distinctive, though not unique in all respects, and to be Christian is to be obliged to follow the distinctive as well as the ordinary morality that is part of a Christian way of life. The ethics of Christians is and must be Christian ethics; all of their moral actions are under Jesus' lordship; since he is Lord, the distinctive aspects of his way of life and teaching are as morally obligatory on those who confess him as Lord as are the ordinary aspects. With some modifications this point of view is present in the early stages of monastic movements (Franciscan morality is one example), in various Anabaptist movements of the sixteenth century, and in "radical" religious movements of the Puritan period (the Quaker movement is one example).

On the basis of a highly restrictive concept of ethics, the latter point of view is not ethics at all; it offers a religious way of life with religious obligations some of which are ethically defensible. The first point of view would, on the basis of a restrictive concept, be ethical throughout until the final justification, the gracious gift of God's creation, is invoked. (Whether "decision is king" only for religious persons at the point of an affirmation or choice either of the "ultimate grounds" of morality or of a definable "way of life" even the philosophers dispute. Certainly it is clear that all moral philosophers, not to mention all rational persons, do not agree on these matters.)

None of these answers to the question, "Can ethics be Christian?" precisely follows from the previous chapters of this book.

A more proper conclusion, stated in most general terms, is that religion *qualifies* morality, and that ethics can be Christian in the senses (*a*) that the morphology of religious morality can be explicated, and (*b*) that certain action-guiding values and principles can be inferred from religious beliefs as normative for those who share some common Christian experience of the reality of God. The religious qualification of morality can be rather thorough in its consequences, but it does not create an exclusive Christian morality or ethics. This general statement will be developed subsequently; it is important to note that the bases for drawing distinctions used in the answers above are not totally applicable to how my conclusions are drawn. Indeed, the basic question of the title must be refined to, "In what senses is it intelligible to speak of ethics as Christian?"

For the sake of organization and economy of words, attention is given here to three crucial aspects of morality that are qualified by Christian experience and belief, and thus three aspects of ethics.[2] They are (1) the reasons for being moral, (2) the character of the moral agent, and (3) the points of reference used to determine conduct.

It is intelligible to speak of morality, and by derivation of ethics, as Christian in the sense that Christianity offers reasons for morality itself, and reasons for persons to be moral. That morality can be interpreted to have other ultimate grounds than Christian theological ones cannot be gainsaid; social conventions, biological necessity, systems of nontheistic metaphysics, and others have been developed. That persons and communities can have reasons for being moral other than those of the Christian faith and tradition is equally uncontradictable; to be happy, to have peace in society, and other reasons have been given. In Christian experience, however, the religious dimensions have priority over the moral. The existence of God is not posited in order to have an ultimate ground for morality; rather the reality of God is experienced, and this experience requires morality; or, by inference from this experience, the reality of God requires morality. One is not a religious person in order to have reasons of mind and heart to be moral; rather, one is religious as a consequence of experience of the reality of God, and this experience requires that one be moral. This conclusion follows from the analysis in chapter 4.

In the religious consciousness of the serious Christian (and I believe also of the devout Jew and Moslem), every moral act is a religiously significant act. To act for the sake of justice for the oppressed is not only a moral act; it is a moral act done for religious as well as moral, indeed for religious-moral reasons, and thus is an act both of fidelity to God and of honor to God. Some Protestant theologians have equivocated on the word "good" to make this point; Luther, for example, believed that an act was truly good only if it was done "in faith." The morally good and the theologically good were collapsed into each other. Such an extreme position does not follow from my analysis. The moral act is qualified by the religious significance it has for the agent in the light of his or her reasons for being moral without collapsing the two references of "good." It is a good act for two distinctive but "overlapping" reasons; it is a morally right or good act because of its consequences or because of the immediate moral principles that governed it. It is also a "good" act for the more ultimate "theological" and "religious" reasons it was done; it was done in fidelity to God, or done to honor God. Since moral intention (for the well-being of creation) is one aspect of the reality of God as experienced, the two distinctive reasons overlap.

If morality is qualified by religion in this sense, then Christian ethics is possible in two aspects. One is making clear the morphology of Christian experience of being moral for "religious" reasons (as I have tried to do). The second is to develop action-guiding principles and values that can be inferred from these reasons; the ethical task is to answer the question, "If one is moral for these reasons, what sorts of moral action ought one to do?" "What values and principles guide the discernment of what God is enabling and requiring me (us) to do?" Theology does not only provide "ultimate grounds" for morality; the morality that it grounds is qualified by the theological beliefs. Christian religious beliefs do not only ground morality; since the reality of God has compelling clarity through Jesus, the morality that it grounds is qualified by that medium. Thus inferences of principles and values, and the ordering of priority of them, are qualified by him.

It is intelligible to speak of morality and ethics as Christian in a second sense, namely, that the experience of God's reality through the Christian "story" qualifies the characteristics or the "characters" of moral agents. That others than Christians have morally commendable characters cannot be contradicted; they emerge from their life experiences and from their commitment to worthy moral values and principles. In Christian experience, however, the religious dimensions have priority over the moral. An experience of God's reality is not sought to prop up moral character; rather, the reality of God is experienced, and with compelling clarity through Jesus; this experience both engenders and requires characteristics of moral agents that are morally commendable. Persons do not worship God, for example, to shore up weaknesses of moral character; rather, to participate in worship is to express and to evoke an experience of the presence of the ultimate power. This experience has consequences for the moral "sort of person" one is becoming. This conclusion follows from the analysis in chapters 2 and 3.

In Christian experience of God and its persisting consequences for persons, it is not possible to separate the "religious" characteristics from the "moral" characteristics of persons. Consciousness cannot be *separated* along a line that distinguishes the moral from the religious. That persons who do not share Christian experience can be loving, hopeful, and faithful cannot be gainsaid; to experience the reality of God with special clarity through the Christian story, however, has, and ought to have, the consequences of nourishing (if not creating) loving, hopeful, and faithful dispositions in Christians. There are "readinesses" to act in certain ways, to seek the interests of others rather than one's own for example, that are nourished and sustained not only by actions in accordance with principles that would direct such action but also by participation in the Christian community with its common memories and its central person. To affirm that dispositions, affections, and intentions of a marked Christian sort are the fruits of Christian experience is not to affirm that other "virtues" like courage and justice are not also nourished by it.

Indeed they are, for the ultimate power whose reality is experienced wills them as well.

If moral agents are qualified by the religious dimensions of experience in this way, then Christian ethics is possible in its two aspects. First, an intelligible account of these qualifications can be rendered, as I have attempted to do. Second, there are imperatives directed toward the sort of persons Christians ought to become that can be inferred from such an account. The normative, like the analytical, task of ethics includes attention to agents as well as acts. This second aspect of the ethical task is to answer the questions, "If one experiences God's reality, particularly informed by the Christian story, what sort of moral person ought one to become?" "What intentions and dispositions ought to be characteristic of Christians?" Quite reasonably, the answer to these questions is likely to resort to illustrations, by pointing to persons whose own life stories seem to embody those characteristics; this is one basis for the imitation of Christ theme in the history of Christian ethics, and for hagiographies both ancient and modern. The sort of person Christians ought to become is informed and influenced (that is, qualified) by the Christian story.[3]

It is intelligible to speak of morality and ethics as Christian in a third sense, namely, that distinctive points of reference are used to give guidance to moral action. These distinctive points of reference function in two ways in Christian moral reflection. First, religious symbols and theological concepts are used to interpret the moral and religious significance of events and circumstances; they are used in the process of forming a descriptive evaluation, or evaluative description, of the occasions for action. That other symbols and concepts can be used no one can dispute, and that the interpretations forthcoming can be accurate in disclosing the crucial moral issues in political, social, or interpersonal circumstances is equally clear. In the Christian community, however, the authorization for the selection of symbols and concepts is not only their potency in disclosing the moral issues; it is also that the confirmation in experience of the power of these symbols and concepts to articulate the experience of God's reality and of man's life in relation to God authorizes their use. These symbols might be highly specific in a historical sense; the use of the cross is one example. What the cross elucidates can be elucidated by other symbols; again, the use of the symbol of the crucifixion is authorized primarily by the compelling clarity it evokes in Christian experience of God as self-giving and self-sacrificing love. This follows from chapter 5.

The second function of distinctive points of reference is to infer and to state action-guiding principles and values that aid the Christian community and its members in discerning what God is enabling and requiring them to be and to do. To find such principles and values is not to guarantee that the actions of Christians are "morally better" than the actions of others whose principles and values are derived from "purely rational" bases. To claim, as the churches seem often to do, that the reason for using Jesus' teachings, or for inferring principles to govern action from theological beliefs, is to develop a "higher" or better morality is a mistake. The prime significance of the Christian experience is its apprehension of God's reality through the Christian story with compelling clarity. A fidelity to God follows which gives distinctive though not exclusive authority to the media through which that experience occurs. Thus there is confidence, though not blind trust, that these historically particular media are a trustworthy basis for finding moral values and principles that are in accord with God's will and reality. This follows from the discussion in chapter 6.

That these values and principles might be distinctive, in the sense that there are claims on the Christian community that appear to be "irrational" and certainly "imprudent" is part of my argument. As we have seen, from a highly restrictive philosophical concept of ethics such claims as that the Christian community ought to be willing to give up its own immediate interests for the sake of others are not moral but religious claims. On the basis of the assumption that certain values and principles have an obligatory character within a "way of life" and that the Christian history and community call for a way of life grounded in the Christian story, it is fitting to call these Christian ethical principles and values. This is clearly not to insist that persons who do not share in that religious way of life must follow those principles or honor those values. While theologically an argument might be made for their universality, the confirmation of their authority is in the history of the Christian community and in personal experience. It is unreasonable to assume that those who do not share the "believing" should be obligated to follow the principles and honor the values that are distinctive to that community. Others may be quite prepared to adhere to these more rigorous demands for other reasons, such as personal ideals or the sustaining ethos of another religious community.[4] But the strength of the claim to engage in such action is qualified by the Christian experience and ethos.

Thus, it is intelligible, and I hope plausible and persuasive, to argue that ethics can be Christian in the senses that have been developed in this book.[5] If the argument is not persuasive, at least it might locate where the crucial issues are. Its import I believe, is not only for ethical theory but also for the Christian communities and churches. They are deeply concerned about human well-being, prone to make moral judgments on all sorts of events, developing rules of behavior and recommendations for policy, and stimulating moral action among their members. All too frequently, however, they are not very clear and precise about the grounds or reasons for their authorizing all this activity.

Epilogue

If my companion of two decades ago in that Lexington Avenue hotel bar were living, with some anxiety I would present him a copy of this book. He would not read it through; to do so would deter him from more important activities even if he had sufficient interest to consider doing so. Perhaps he would glance through it and, with smiling amusement, thank me.

Obviously I hold him in deep admiration; obviously I found his course of action to be morally praiseworthy. I could, I suppose, call him an "anonymous Christian," but that would be imperious on my part, and insulting to him. What he did that night, and indeed on many other occasions, was the sort of thing Christians ought to do under similar circumstances. Perhaps that is why our common experience is unforgettable to me.

If readers now ask, "If this is the case, then why be religious or Christian?" they have missed the basic point of the book. If one is Christian or religious in order to be moral, just as if one is Christian in order to be happy, the heart of religion is not yet grasped. The heart of religion is the experience of the reality of God, mediated through all sorts of other experiences. The distinctiveness of the Christian experience of the reality of God is that he is experienced with compelling clarity in Jesus and in the Christian story. The confirmation of this (not an uncritical one) in experience grounds Christian morality. Christian ethics is the intellectual discipline that renders an account of this experience and that draws the normative inferences from it for the conduct of the Christian community and its members. The practical import is to aid the community and its members in discerning what God is enabling and requiring them to be and to do.

That my companion was not religious in no way detracts from his moral worthiness. But that many of us are religious, but not as worthy as he, is both a moral and religious judgment on us.

Notes

Chapter 1

1. H. Richard Niebuhr, *The Responsible Self* (New York: Harper and Row, 1963), p. 52.

2. Ibid., p. 48.

3. Hannah Arendt, *The Human Condition* (Chicago: University of Chicago Press, 1958), pp. 153-59.

4. Niebuhr, p. 56.

5. Arendt, p. 232.

6. I once published a typology based upon "character" rather than upon patterns of decision and action: the conventional moral man, the rebel, the drifter, the do-gooder, the moral realist, the less-than-moral realist, the double life, the exemplary man, the moral coward, the indignant moral man, the vicarious moral man, and the moral virtuoso. See James M. Gustafson, "Types of Moral Life," *Religious Education* 57 (Nov.-Dec. 1962: 403-10.

Chapter 2

1. For more extensive discussion, see James M. Gustafson, "The Christian Style of Life: Problematics of a Good Idea," *Una Sancta* 24 (1967): 6-14; reprinted in Gustafson, *Christian Ethics and the Community* (Philadelphia: United Church Press, 1971), pp. 177-85.

2. Some recent pertinent books are: John MacMurray, *The Self as Agent* (New York: Harper, 1957); John MacMurray, *Persons in Relation* (New York: Harper, 1961); G. E. M. Anscombe, *Intention,* 2d ed. (Oxford: B. Blackwell, 1963); Stuart Hampshire, *Thought and Action* (New York: Viking, 1960); Eric D'Arcy, *Human Acts* (Oxford: Clarendon Press, 1963); Richard Taylor, *Action and Purpose* (Englewood Cliffs: Prentice-Hall, 1966); R. S. Peters, *The Concept of Motivation* (London: Routledge and Kegan Paul, 1960); Anthony Kenny, *Action, Emotion and Will* (London: Routledge and Kegan Paul, 1963); Paul Ricoeur, *Freedom and Nature: The Voluntary and the Involuntary* (Evanston: Northwestern University Press, 1966); and Talcott Parsons and Edward Shils, eds., *Toward a General Theory of Action* (Cambridge: Harvard University Press, 1952). Among recent collections of essays are: Sidney Hook, ed., *Determinism and Freedom in the Age of Modern Science* (New York: Collier Books, 1961); Bernard Berofsky, ed., *Free Will and Determinism* (New York: Harper and Row,

1966); and Keith Lehrer, ed., *Freedom and Determinism* (New York: Random House, 1966).

3. Ray L. Hart, *Unfinished Man and the Imagination* (New York: Herder and Herder, 1968), esp. pp. 125-62. Novel terms often evoke insight in a way that tired ones no longer do, but whether their use reconceptualizes the problem is not so clear to me.

4. Peters, p. 37.

5. George P. Klubertanz, S. J., *Habits and Virtues* (New York: Appleton-Century-Crofts, 1965), p. 101.

6. I have published two short accounts of these matters previously; a more detailed and technical development remains to be done. See James M. Gustafson, "What Ought I to Do?" *Proceedings of the American Catholic Philosophical Association* 43 (1969): 56-70, and "Education for Moral Responsibility," in Nancy F. and Theodore R. Sizer, eds., *Moral Education: Five Lectures* (Cambridge: Harvard University Press, 1970), pp. 11-27.

7. Karl Rahner presses for a maximal position on the issue of the extent to which the person's capacities for self-determination can govern what others judge to be conditions to which man merely consents. He is concerned to avoid those divisions that "would ontologically and ethically split up the one person." "He draws his life out of soil and roots whose quality he comes to recognize only slowly and never adequately. He cannot say that all this does not concern him, as if the 'this' and the 'he' were two distinct things and the 'he' can be held responsible only for 'himself,' provided this 'himself' is strictly identical with this 'he.' " "Some Thought on 'A Good Intention,' " in Rahner, *Theological Investigations* 3, (Baltimore: Helicon Press, 1967): p. 117.

8. The literature on excusing conditions is fairly large. There are writers who minimize the distinction between what is excusable and what is not. For example, John Hospers writes in the course of his argument, "Let us note that the more *thoroughly* and *in detail* we know the causal factors leading a person to behave as he does, the more we tend to exempt him from responsibility." See his "What Means This Freedom?" in Sidney Hook, ed., *Determinism and Freedom,* pp. 126-42, quotation from p. 133; see also Paul Edwards's essay, pp. 117-25, and Hook's response to both, pp. 187-92, in the same volume. From the perspective of the law, see in the same volume H. L. A. Hart's "Legal Responsibility and Excuses," pp. 95-116.

9. See Erikson's discussion in *Insight and Responsibility* (New York: Norton, 1964), chap. 4.

10. Jürgen Moltmann, *Theology of Hope* (New York: Harper and Row, 1967), chap.3.

11. The literature pertinent to this discussion continues to grow. Some of the more relevant books are cited in note 2 above.

12. The literature is rather large on the matter of belief. Three quite different sorts of treatment are: H. H. Price, *Belief* (New York: Humanities Press, 1970); Michael Polanyi, *Personal Knowledge* (London: Routledge and Kegan Paul, 1958), chap. 10, "Commitment," pp. 299-324; and Van A. Harvey, *The Historian and the Believer* (New York: Macmillan, 1966).

13. Aristotle *Nicomachean Ethics* 2.1. Cf. Plato's discussion in "Meno."

14. Romano Guardini, *The Virtues: On Forms of Moral Life* (Chicago: Regnery, 1967), p. 2.

15. St. Thomas Aquinas, *Summa Theologica,* I-II, Q. 54, art. 3.

16. Maurice Mandelbaum, *The Phenomenology of Moral Experience* (Glencoe, Ill.; Free Press, 1955), p. 177.

17. For one of many treatments, see Anthony Kenny, *Action, Emotion and Will,* cited in n. 2 above.

18. Jonathan Edwards, *Religious Affections* (New Haven: Yale University Press, 1959), pp. 96-99; see also John E. Smith's Introduction to this edition, pp. 12 ff.

19. Kenny, *Action, Emotion and Will,* p. 63.

20. Hart, *Unfinished Man and the Imagination,* pp. 147-48.

21. Ibid., pp. 148-53.

22. Hampshire, *Thought and Action,* p. 125.

Chapter 3

1. Arend T. van Leeuwen's book by this title, *Christianity and World History* (New York: Scribners, 1964), had a considerable impact upon the theological discussions of secularization.

2. Erik H. Erikson, *Insight and Responsibility: Lectures on the Ethical Implications of Psychoanalytical Insight* (New York: Norton, 1964), p. 115.

3. Ibid., p. 116. Erikson's italics.

4. Ibid., p. 118. Erikson's italics.

5. William F. Lynch, *Images of Hope* (Baltimore: Helicon Press, 1965), p. 32, "... hope is, in its most general terms, a sense of *the possible.*" The entire discussion is extraordinarily perceptive. See also James M. Gustafson, "The Conditions of Hope: Reflections on Human Experience," *Continuum* 7 (Winter 1970): 535-45, reprinted in Gustafson, *Christian Ethics and the Community* (Philadelphia: Pilgrim Press, 1971), pp. 205-16.

6. I have attempted to delineate this process of being influenced and informed by the gospel accounts of Jesus Christ in "The Relation of the Gospels to Moral Life," in Donald G. Miller and D. Y. Hadidian, eds., *Jesus and Man's Hope* (Pittsburgh: Pittsburgh Theological Seminary, 1971), 2:103-17.

7. James B. Nelson, *Moral Nexus: Ethics of Christian Identity and Community* (Philadelphia: Westminster Press, 1971). See also James M. Gustafson, *Treasure in Earthen Vessels: The Church as a Human Community* (New York: Harper, 1961), chaps. 4-7.

8. My own reflections on the answers to these questions has been informed by a great variety of literature in philosophy and in theology. Four recent contributions have been especially suggestive: John E. Smith, *Experience and God* (New York: Oxford University Press, 1968); Julian N. Hartt, "Encounter and Inference in Our Awareness of God," in Joseph P. Whelan, S.J., *The Experience of God* (New York: Newman Press, 1971), pp. 30-59; Richard R. Niebuhr, *Experiential Religion* (New York: Harper and Row, 1972); and Dallas M. High, *Language, Persons, and Belief* (New York: Oxford University Press, 1967).

9. See Victor P. Furnish, *The Love Command in the New Testament* (Nashville; Abingdon Press, 1972). See also his *Theology and Ethics in Paul* (Nashville: Abingdon Press, 1968). These books have the value not only of expressing Furnish's own arguments and judgments but of bringing to the reader whose specialty is not New Testament scholarship a wealth of material developed by many scholars with whom Furnish is in dialogue.

10. In an essay, "Religion and Morality in Theological Perspective" in a volume edited by Gene Outka and John P. Reeder (*Religion and Morality* [New York: Doubleday, 1973]), I have attempted to develop salient features of the relationship between the two with reference to some important religious texts in both Judaism and Christianity. The purpose of the article is to indicate that logical distinctions between the two as these are made by contemporary philosophers founder on the texts because of certain distinctive aspects of theology in the two traditions.

11. Hartt, "Encounter and Inference in Our Awareness of God," p. 52.

12. H. Richard Niebuhr, *Christ and Culture* (New York: Harper, 1951), p. 17.

13. Both Julian N. Hartt and Richard R. Niebuhr make a sense of a power over against man to be at the heart of religion. "We ought to say that man is not really religious unless he feels that some power is bearing down on him, unless, that is, he believes that he must do something about divine powers who have done something about him," is Hartt's statement in his *A Christian Critique of American Culture* (New York: Harper and Row, 1967), p. 52. After listing various views of "human religiousness," Niebuhr states that "the link among them all [is] basic human responsiveness of power.... Religion arises as human reaction and answer to the state of being affected totally." R. R. Niebuhr, *Experiential Religion,* p. 34.

14. John E. Smith, *Experience and God,* pp. 52, 53. See also Langdon Gilkey, *Naming the Whirlwind* (Indianapolis: Bobbs-Merrill, 1969), pp. 305-413.

15. I have borrowed Hartt's language and ideas and absorbed them for my purposes. He has one of the most brilliant and profound theological minds and spirits in the Christian community today; unfortunately he is one of the least appreciated theologians now writing.

16. An analysis of the answers to these questions in detail, and with powerful analytical equipment as the answers have been given in theology, can be found in Gene Outka, *Agape* (New Haven: Yale University Press, 1972).

17. Professor Hauerwas of Notre Dame has aided me in clarifying this pattern of thought. After intensive and intricate analysis of historical and contemporary texts, he defines "character" as "the qualification and determination of man's self-agency through which his life acquires continuity, direction, and orientation." See "Summary" and throughout, in Stanley Martin Hauerwas, "Moral Character as a Problem for Theological Ethics" Ph.D. diss., Yale University, 1968.

18. See W. D. Davies, *The Setting of the Sermon on the Mount* (Cambridge: Cambridge University Press, 1964) pp. 94-99. Davies musters evidence to show that in Matthew's gospel there is great continuity with the Jewish Torah tradition. This brief section on the Christian life in the first gospel indicates what some aspects of life under Christ's Lordship are.

19. John Noonan, in Noonan, ed., *The Morality of Abortion* (Cambridge: Harvard University Press, 1970), p. 59.

20. See K. E. Kirk's excellent historical account of this in *The Vision of God* (London: Longmans, Green, 1931).

21. The interpretation of St. Augustine's view of love is the subject of an extensive literature, some of which develops distinctions and refinements more precise than are needed for our purposes. See, for example, John Burnaby, *Amor Dei* (London: Hodder and Stoughton, 1938), and particularly his arguments against Anders Nygren, pp. 15-19. See also Kirk's discussion in *The Vision of God*, pp. 319-46.

22. St. Augustine, *Confessions*, bk. 13, ch. 9, Everymans Library edition (New York: Dutton, 1946), p. 315. Cf. St. Thomas Aquinas, for example, *Summa Theologica*, I-II Q. 26, art. 1, " 'Love' denotes that which produces the inclination to move towards the end in question."

23. St. Augustine, *The City of God,* bk. 14, ch. 7, Modern Library edition (New York: Random House, 1950), p. 449.

24. Ibid., bk. 19, ch. 13, p. 690.

25. See H. R. Niebuhr, *Christ and Culture,* chap. 6.

26. F. D. E. Schleiermacher, *The Christian Faith* (Edinburgh: T. and T. Clark, 1928), p. 524.

Chapter 4

1. I believe such inquiries are worthwhile and important; exclusion here is a practical matter. For a recent critique of moral philosophies that do not include ontological dimensions, see Henry B. Veatch, *For an Ontology of Morals* (Evanston: Northwestern University Press, 1971). For a careful account in a generally Kantian outlook, see W. G. Maclagen, *The Theological Frontiers of Ethics* (London: George Allen and Unwin, 1961); for an intensive critique of Maclagen from a more confessional Christian perspective see N. H. G. Robinson, *The Groundwork of Christian Ethics* (Grand Rapids, Mich.: Eerdmans, 1971), pp. 79-99.

2. See William Frankena, "Is Morality Logically Dependent on Religion?" in Gene Outka and John P. Reeder, eds., *Religion and Morality* (New York: Doubleday, 1973), pp. 295-317.

3. The following section is a revision and extension of a pattern I used in my Bellarmine Lecture delivered at St. Louis University in October 1971, published as "Spiritual Life and Moral Life," *Theology Digest* 19 (Winter 1971): 296-307. Used with permission.

Chapter 5

1. See, for example, Gustavo Gutierrez, *A Theology of Liberation* (Maryknoll, N.Y.: Orbis Books, 1973), and Frederick Herzog, *Liberation Theology* (New York: Seabury Press, 1972). The formal pattern could also be worked out with reference to hope and other concepts.

2. See, for example, Richard M. Shaull, "Christian Theology and Social Revolution (I)," *Perkins School of Theology Journal* 21 (1968): 11-12.

3. See for example, the discussion of this symbol in Phillip E. Berryman, "Latin American Liberation Theology," *Theological Studies* 34 (1973): 388.

4. Paul Lehmann, *Ethics in a Christian Context* (New York: Harper and Row, 1963), chap. 3.

5. Paul VI, *On the Development of Peoples*, 26 March 1967.

6. See, for example, Reinhold Niebuhr, *Christianity and Power Politics* (New York: Scribners, 1946), chap. 4-6, 8-10. See Emanuel Hirsch, *Deutschlands Schicksal* (Göttingen: Vanderhoeck und Ruprecht, 1925), especially pp. 79-93, and Paul Althaus, *Theologie der Ordnungen* (Gütersloh: C. Bertelsmann, 1935). For Althaus and others there were also critical principles for judging particular orders.

7. See, for example, Karl Barth, *Church Dogmatics*, III/2 (Edinburgh: T. and T. Clark, 1960), pp. 132-202, and Dietrich Bonhoeffer, *Ethics* (London: S. C. M. Press, 1955), pp. 55-62, who use the terms "reality" and "real" in a strong sense. I do not wish to defend such a strong claim, but only one that claims a special or distinctive significance. For a theological interpretation it is the most important significance, but this does not warrant immodest claims for access to the "real" significance.

8. Arthur Schlesinger, Jr., "Reinhold Niebuhr's Role in American Political Thought and Life," in Charles W. Kegley and Robert W. Bretall, eds., *Reinhold Niebuhr: His Religious, Social, and Political Thought* (New York: Macmillan, 1956), pp. 126-50.

9. H. Richard Niebuhr, "War as the Judgment of God," *Christian Century* 59 (1942): 630-33, and "War as Crucifixion," ibid. 60 (1943): 513-15.

10. "War as the Judgment of God," p. 630.

11. For that, see H. R. Niebuhr, *The Meaning of Revelation* (New York, Macmillan, 1941).

12. "War as Crucifixion," p. 513.

13. "War as the Judgment of God," p. 631.

14. Ibid., p. 632.

15. This synopsis is not unfair to Karl Barth; for ways in which he interprets events in its light see *Church Dogmatics* III/4 throughout and occasional essays such as in *How to Serve God in a Marxist Land*, by Barth and J. Hamel (New York: Association Press, 1959).

16. I have noted this conversation also in "The Place of Scripture in Christian Ethics: A Methodological Study," *Interpretation* 24 (1970): 430-55.

17. Many of my theological and philosophical colleagues would use the term hermeneutics to cover much of what I am referring to in this chapter.

18. See John Howard Yoder, *The Politics of Jesus* (Grand Rapids, Mich.: Eerdmans, 1972), for an argument that Jesus was a nonviolent but aggressive resister to social oppression; see also Yoder's extensive and valuable accounts of New Testament scholarship related negatively and positively to his thesis.

19. A similar problem could be analyzed in Teilhard de Chardin's theological interpretation of the significance of the evolutionary process. He appears to claim

that a scientific interpretation of that process makes plausible his application to it of concepts like "Christification" and "amorization." But in the final analysis, the authorization of these concepts is a theological one, and their specification fits a larger theological system. But why use these concepts to interpret evolution? Why not some other theological symbols, like man's sin? These questions are answerable from de Chardin's writing; I merely want to alert the reader to the importance of being conscious of them. If sin, rather than "Christification," were the dominant concept, the human biological future would have been prognosticated differently, and a different basic attitude would have been called for. Also, different courses of action would follow. See Pierre Teilhard de Chardin, *The Phenomenon of Man* (New York: Harper Torchbooks, 1952).

20. See J. Moltmann, *Theology of Hope* (New York: Harper and Row, 1967); Wolfhart Pannenberg, *Theology and the Kingdom of God* (Philadelphia: Westminster Press, 1969) (chap. 3 is important for ethics); and Carl F. Braaten, *The Future of God* (New York: Harper and Row, 1969).

21. Within the process theological movement, this is done in different ways. Compare, for example, Daniel Day Williams, *The Spirit and the Forms of Love* (New York: Harper and Row, 1968), in which the process concepts are used primarily to elucidate some traditional Christian doctrines, with John Cobb, *A Christian Natural Theology* (Philadelphia: Westminster Press, 1965), which makes the Whiteheadian philosophy in control and seeks to spell out implication of it for Christian thinking.

Chapter 6

1. See James M. Gustafson, "Two Approaches to Theological Ethics," *Union Seminary Quarterly Review* 22 (1968): 337–48, reprinted in Gustafson, *Christian Ethics and the Community* (Philadelphia: Pilgrim Press, 1971), pp. 127–38, for an earlier discussion of mine on this matter.

2. See Karl Barth, *Church Dogmatics* II/2 (Edinburgh: T. and T. Clark, 1957), pp. 509–781; H. Richard Niebuhr, *The Responsible Self* (New York: Harper and Row, 1963); and the articles cited in chapter 5 above; Paul Lehmann, *Ethics in a Christian Context* (New York: Harper and Row, 1963); and Emil Brunner, *The Divine Imperative* (Philadelphia: Westminster Press, 1947). Brunner combines a doctrine of orders of creation with these elements; this accounts for the qualification in the text.

3. See Niebuhr, "War as the Judgment of God," *Christian Century* 59 (1942): 630, and Paul Lehmann, "The Foundation and Pattern of Christian Behavior," in John A. Hutchinson, ed., *Christian Faith and Social Action* (New York: Scribners, 1953), p. 100. Lehmann's words are, "What does God do?"

4. I use the notion of "type" in a technical sense; it is an ideal construct based upon diverse texts, but not a summary generalization of them. It is intentionally simple and does not account for important differences among the authors. It is a proper type if it enables persons to "see" crucial aspects of the texts to which it can be applied.

5. I have dealt more thoroughly with relations of Catholic and Protestant ethics in my Hoover Lectures, delivered in January 1972, at the University of Chicago, and my Touhy Lectures delivered at John Carroll University in the same month. These lectures are under revision for publication.

6. See, for example, St. Thomas Aquinas, *Summa Theologica,* II-II, Q. 64, art. 5., where he invokes Augustine's explanation of Samson's suicide. For extensive discussion of these "exceptions" to the natural law in Aquinas, see John Giles Milhaven, "Moral Absolutes and Thomas Aquinas," in Charles Curran, ed., *Absolutes in Moral Theology?* (Washington: Corpus Books, 1968), pp. 154-85. For an argument that all scripturally described moral actions are in principle subject to rational defense, see Bruno Schüller, S.J., "Zur Problematik Allgemein Verbindliches Ethisches Grundsätz," *Theologie und Philosophie* 54 (1970): 1-23.

7. The secondary sources on Luther's ethics are many. I have treated them with another intention in James M. Gustafson, *Christ and the Moral Life* (New York: Harper and Row, 1968), pp. 120-30. I find Gustaf Wingren's development of them in *Luther on Vocation* (Philadelphia: Muhlenberg Press, 1957), to be sound and balanced. See also George Forell, *Faith Active in Love* (New York: American Press, 1954), and Paul Althaus, *The Ethics of Martin Luther* (Philadelphia: Fortress Press, 1972).

8. N. H. G. Robinson, *Groundwork of Christian Ethics* (Grand Rapids, Mich.: Eerdmans, 1972), p. 22. For pertinent recent American discussion of Calvin's ethics, see David Little, *Religion, Order and Law* (New York: Harper Torchbooks, 1969), and Arthur C. Cochrane, "Natural Law in Calvin," in Elwyn A. Smith, ed., *Church-State Relations in Ecumenical Perspective* (Pittsburgh: Duquesne University Press, 1966), pp. 176-217.

9. Calvin, *Institutes,* II, chap. 8, secs. 1 and 7.

10. See Frederick Carney, "Accountability in Christian Morality," *Journal of Religion* 53 (1973): 309-29, for an excellent analysis of how it is defensible to speak of Christian ethics in this sense.

11. Reinhold Niebuhr, *Faith and History* (New York: Scribners, 1949), pp. 174-75, and elsewhere.

12. Walter Rauschenbusch, *The Social Principles of Jesus* (New York: Association Press, 1917), p. 128. See my discussion of his use of scripture in James M. Gustafson, "From Scripture to Social Policy and Social Action," *Andover Newton Quarterly* 9 (1969): 160-69.

13. Paul Ramsey, *War and the Christian Conscience* (Durham, N.C.: Duke University Press, 1961), p. 190. My point stretches this citation, but I believe it is valid for Ramsey's work.

14. See Rauschenbusch, *Christianizing the Social Order* (New York: Macmillan, 1912); J. C. Bennett, *Christian Ethics and Social Policy* (New York: Scribners, 1946); and Paul Ramsey, "The Case of the Curious Exception," in Gene Outka and Paul Ramsey, eds., *Norm and Context in Christian Ethics* (New York: Scribners, 1968), pp. 67-135. I have discussed these authors in previous publications, and thus do not expand on the materials here. See J. M. Gustafson,

Christian Ethics and the Community (Philadelphia: Pilgrim Press, 1971), chaps. 1 and 3.

15. See, for example, John Howard Yoder, *The Politics of Jesus* (Grand Rapids, Mich.: Eerdmans, 1972).

16. My article, "Moral Discernment in the Christian Life," in Outka and Ramsey, eds., *Norm and Context in Christian Ethics*, pp. 17-36, was an earlier effort to state a personal position. This constructive proposal has been ignored by others far more than a number of my analytical articles. Perhaps I should have learned something from that!

17. See, for example, his definition of a theonomous conscience in *Ethics in a Christian Context* (New York: Harper and Row, 1963), pp. 258-59.

18. The language of a "way of life" has interestingly achieved a dignity and currency in some contemporary moral philosophy. See R. M. Hare, *The Language of Morals* (Oxford: Oxford University Press, 1954), p. 69. Also Paul W. Taylor, *Normative Discourse* (Englewood Cliffs, N. J.: Prentice Hall, 1961), pp. 151-58.

19. See John Howard Yoder, *The Politics of Jesus,* for one argument supporting this.

Chapter 7

1. The Christology, the ethics, and the relations of the church to the world involved in this point of view are those of Ernst Troeltshch's "Church-type"; those involved in the second are his "sect-type." See Ernst Troeltsch, *The Social Teaching of the Christian Churches* (Glencoe, Ill.: Free Press, 1949), I, pp. 331-43.

2. The order of introduction here differs from the order of the chapters. There I followed what appeared to me (though it may not to all readers) an order that followed from experience, emerging from the illustration in chapter 1.

3. See James M. Gustafson, "The Relation of the Gospels to Moral Life," in Donald G. Miller and D. Y. Hadidian, eds., *Jesus and Man's Hope* (Pittsburgh: Pittsburgh Theological Seminary, 1971), 2: 103-17.

4. See, for example, L. Jacobs, "Greater Love Hath No Man... The Jewish Point of View on Self-Sacrifice," *Judaism* 6 (1957): 41-47.

5. I believe the formal pattern of my analysis will bear the weight of a more inclusive range of materials. Thus, ethics can be "religious" in this way, when religion refers to generalizations based either on the characteristics of various historical religions or on some "generic" or functional concept of religion. Further, the formal pattern might function as a basis for "comparative" religious ethics. My own research has concentrated on Catholic and Protestant ethics, with Jewish ethics and law increasingly in view; I am not competent to make a range beyond these. Other scholars, happily among them are former students and colleagues of mine, are gaining the competence to do such work. See, for example, David Little, "Comparative Religious Ethics," in Paul Ramsey and John F. Wilson, eds., *The Study of Religion in Colleges and Universities* (Princeton: Princeton University Press, 1970), pp. 216-45.

Index